The Irish Aesthete
Ruins of Ireland

The Irish Aesthete
Ruins of Ireland

Robert O'Byrne

CICO BOOKS

LONDON NEW YORK

Published in 2019 by CICO Books
An imprint of Ryland Peters & Small Ltd
20–21 Jockey's Fields   341 E 116th St
London WC1R 4BW   New York, NY 10029

www.rylandpeters.com

10 9 8 7 6 5 4 3 2 1

A CIP catalog record for this book is available from the
Library of Congress and the British Library.

ISBN: 978 1 78249 686 1

Printed in China

Editor: Lisa Pendreigh
Designer: Geoff Borin
Photographer: Robert O'Byrne

In-house editor: Anna Galkina
Art director: Sally Powell
Head of production: Patricia Harrington
Publishing manager: Penny Craig
Publisher: Cindy Richards

Illustrations:
Front cover: Mount Shannon, County Limerick
Back cover, left to right: Loughcrew, County Meath
    and Bunowen Castle, County Galway
Endpapers: Lackeen, County Tipperary
Page 1: Lakeview, County Cork
Pages 2–3: New Hall, County Clare
Page 4: Dromdiah, County Cork
Page 7: Carstown Manor, County Louth
Pages 8–9: Dunmoe Castle, County Meath and Louth
    Hall, County Louth,
Pages 62–63: Ardtully, County Kerry and
    Ballysaggartmore Towers, County Waterford
Pages 116–117: Roscommon Castle, County
    Roscommon and Clonfert Palace, County Galway
Pages 144–145: Shane's Castle, County Antrim and
Raphoe Palace, County Donegal

Contents

Introduction

In 1842, German writer and geographer Johann Georg Kohl traveled around Ireland, publishing an account of his journey the following year. "Of all the countries in the world," he observed, "Ireland is the country for ruins. Here you have ruins of every period of history, from the time of the Phoenicians down to the present day... down to our own times each century has marked its progress by the ruins it has left. Nay, every decade, one might almost say, has set its sign upon Ireland, for in all directions you see a number of dilapidated buildings, ruins of yesterday's erection." *

Little has changed over the intervening 180-odd years. If anything, the sheer quantity of ruins has only increased, especially among buildings of the kind featured here. When the late Mark Bence-Jones produced his still-invaluable *A Guide to Irish Country Houses* in 1978, he estimated that at the start of the twentieth century there had been in the region of 2,000 such properties. Today the number is infinitely smaller, and still shrinking.

It used to be popularly thought that the majority of lost Irish country houses were burnt during the Troubles of the early 1920s. In fact, while several hundred did suffer this fate, many more were unroofed, abandoned, or pulled down over the following decades as public indifference, and sometimes active hostility (the houses were seen as symbols of a widely-detested landlord class), combined with high taxation and low incomes made their maintenance in private hands impossible. In the 1940s and '50s, as in many other parts of the world, country houses disappeared at an alarming rate.

One of the differences between Ireland and other western European states is that her stock of heritage properties continues to decline. Despite efforts to establish one, there is no equivalent of Britain's National Trust and National Trust for Scotland, and this has had unhappy consequences. Thirty years ago, the Irish Architectural Archive and Irish Georgian Society jointly produced a "melancholy catalogue of loss," *Vanishing Country Houses of Ireland*. Were a new edition to be produced today, it would require an addendum. It is true some country houses look assured of a secure future, not least those taken into state care, but others remain at risk: a few examples of such places are included in this book. Although extensive legislation intended to protect buildings listed as historically significant exists on Irish statute books, the law is rarely applied. As a consequence, the owner of a listed house can—and sometimes does—allow it to fall into dereliction, confident there will be no official retribution.

Tumbling roofs and crumbling walls of course exert their own appeal, as was noted by Rose Macaulay in her 1953 book *Pleasure of Ruins* when she rhetorically enquired "what part is played by morbid pleasure in decay, by righteous pleasure in retribution..." The morbidity of ruins without doubt helps to explain their attraction. In a state of decay, they allow us engage in romantic speculation which may or may not be accurate: *Roma quanta fuit ipsa ruina docet* (How great Rome was, its ruins tell).

"To delight in the aspects of *sentient* ruin might appear a heartless pastime," Henry James acknowledged in *Italian Hours* (1873) "and the pleasure, I confess, shows the note of perversity." It is easy to revel in ruins, but there is also the matter of aesthetic beauty: some ruins are wonderfully picturesque, a fact noted by late eighteenth-century writers such as William Gilpin. Even Kohl, much as he disapproved of the excessive abundance of dereliction across the country, had to admit "Irish ruins generally wear a very picturesque look."

Nevertheless, one should resist succumbing to the siren call of a "good" ruin. The fact is that in too many cases Ireland's ample stock of ruined country houses represents nothing more than shameful neglect, and failure to appreciate the craftsmanship of our forebears. By allowing them to perish, we not only disrespect the work of previous generations, we also lose part of our shared history. Ireland remains a country of ruins, but the hope must be that their number no longer continues to rise.

* *Travels in Ireland* by Johann Georg Kohl (1843).

CHAPTER 1

LEINSTER

Since the early seventeenth century, Ireland has been divided into four provinces (previously there had been more.) Today the provinces have no official or administrative purpose, but continue to define the country in areas like sport. Leinster largely occupies the eastern side of the country, and is centered on Dublin. The capital's dominance means this is by far the most densely populated region: according to the 2016 census, over 2.6 million people live in Leinster, more than a third of the total for the entire island. But the province has always had a strong presence, not least thanks to the quality of its agricultural land which over centuries was able to sustain a substantial population. Good land also meant that Leinster could support more country houses than elsewhere. Many of these survive but, as can be seen over the coming pages, many have been lost over hundreds of years due to war and social upheaval, and some remain at risk.

Castleboro

COUNTY WEXFORD

The Carew family are known to have settled in County
Wexford during the first half of the seventeenth century.
Ultimately their estate ran to more than 20,000 acres
and was centered on a house called Ballyboro: this was
changed to Castleboro in 1770. The building appears
to have undergone various incarnations before being
largely destroyed by fire in the early 1840s, after which
its owner Robert Shapland Carew, recently ennobled as
first Baron Carew, spent the considerable sum of £84,000
on constructing a palatial new house, completed in
1848. Castleboro, which is said to have been visited on
several occasions by Queen Victoria, was famous for its
terraced gardens and fountains. However with the onset
of Ireland's War of Independence, the family considered
it best to leave the country and move to England, taking
at least some of Castleboro's contents with them: the
rest was sold off at auction. In early February 1923,
Irish Republican Army irregulars broke into the house,
soaked bales of hay in paraffin, and then lit them, so that
only a shell was left. This single-storey lodge, marking
the entrance of a new approach to Castleboro through
its parkland, dates from the 1860s and was evidently
intended to provide advance notice of the main house's
grandeur. Built in local granite and featuring an elegant
Doric portico, the building looks set soon to vanish into
the encroaching vegetation.

Arch Hall COUNTY MEATH

So many questions about Arch Hall remain the subject of speculation. Who was the architect? When was it built? And for whom? The house's design is usually attributed to Sir Edward Lovett Pearce (c.1699–1733), as is that of the strikingly similar (and likewise now ruined) Wardtown Castle, County Donegal (see page 150). The building is believed to derive its name from a rustic arch lying some distance to the south of the house and serving as point of access to the original avenue. Placed on an axis and intended to offer an unexpected vista of the property, the arch is composed of a single broad entrance with pinnacle above and flanking buttresses. From this point Arch Hall looks like a substantial building, but the impression is deceptive. Despite rising three storeys over the basement, the house was only one room deep. Its dominant feature is the nine-bay façade, concluding on either side in cylindrical bows, and centered on a larger,

three-bay semi-circular bow. This has a handsome stone pedimented Gibbsian doorcase, but the rest of the building was constructed of locally-produced red brick. At some—also unknown—date in the nineteenth century, the exterior was covered in cement render marked out to imitate cut stone. A painting from 1854 by Yorkshire-born artist James Walsham Baldock depicts the wife of Arch Hall's then-owner Samuel Garnett and the couple's two young sons on horseback with the house visible behind. At the time, it was surrounded by a belt of mature trees but most of these have now gone, leaving the building isolated and even more exposed to the elements than would otherwise be the case. The next generation of the family suffered successive tragedies, as one child after another died and then finally in 1923 the house itself was burnt. Since then it has stood abandoned and has fallen into ruin.

The date of Arch Hall's construction is a mystery, as is its architect. In the early eighteenth century the townland of which it is part, Newtown-Clongill was owned by the Payne or Pain(e) family, and therefore the assumption must be that they commissioned the building.

Glyde Court
COUNTY LOUTH

In 1776, John Thomas Foster of Rosy Park, County Louth married Lady Elizabeth Hervey, youngest daughter of Frederick Hervey, Bishop of Derry and Earl of Bristol. Although they had three children, two of whom survived to adulthood, the union was not a success and the couple separated after five years. What followed next is well known. Lady Elizabeth moved to England where, in 1782, she met the Duke and Duchess of Devonshire in Bath. Soon she and the Duchess, the famous Lady Georgiana Spencer, had become close friends. Subsequently Lady Elizabeth became a mistress of the Duke with whom she had two children. Although both born elsewhere in Europe, the pair were eventually brought to England and raised with the Devonshires' own offspring. Lady Elizabeth is also believed to have been the mistress of several other notable figures including the Dukes of Dorset and Richmond, Count Axel von Fersen, and the first Earl of Dunraven. In 1809, three years after the death of Georgiana, she married the Duke of Devonshire but within two years he too had died. Eventually she moved to Rome and remained there until her own death in 1824. Meanwhile, her first husband had remained in this house, subsequently renamed Glyde Court, with the couple's two sons who he forbade to see their mother for the next fourteen years. The Fosters continued to occupy Glyde Court until the 1960s, since when the house has gradually fallen into ruin.

Left and overleaf *Glyde Court's appearance today is very different from the house which Lady Elizabeth Hervey would have known. In the first half of the nineteenth century, the eighteenth-century classical building was transformed into a neo-Jacobean mansion but elements like the bow windows hark back to its earlier incarnation.*

Belan COUNTY KILDARE

In January 1908 the *Journal of the Kildare Archaeological Society* published the reminiscences of the elderly Georgina Sartoris, recalling her visits to Belan some seventy years earlier as a little girl. It was, she recalled, "a fine stone mansion, a magnificent flight of granite steps, with two stone vases at the top, led to the entrance door. Though uninhabited for fully ten years, the house was in perfect repair, no trace of damp or decay and to all appearance, might have been lived in a week before. I have not a distinct recollection of all the rooms; but the dining room is fresh in my memory, also the saloon, and his late lordship's bedroom. The dining room, not very large was panelled, family portraits being set in the panelling. I was too young to care much about them, but feel sure they were all of men. Had there been lovely ladies or pretty children amongst them, I should

have remembered them. The saloon was lovely, with a polished floor of narrow oak boards… on one occasion (why I know not) my sister and myself occupied his late lordship's bedroom, very comfortable it was of moderate size, the fireplace like those of the other bedrooms surrounded with the prettiest tiles I have ever seen, the ground white with pink and blue landscapes, figures and flowers on it; a fine four post mahogany bedstead, Indian chintz curtains, some Chippendale chairs, and a wardrobe are all I remember of its furniture…" During the course of her life, Georgina witnessed Belan, once home to the Earls of Aldborough, gradually fall into decay. The "fine stone mansion" was demolished in the 1940s and today, aside from a handful of follies in the former parkland, only this section of the stable yard survives.

Carbury Castle stands at the heart of an ancient territory known as Cairbre Uí Chiardha, associated with a sept of the Uí Néill clan from which Niall of the Nine Hostages, a famous fourth-century king, was supposed to have been descended. The name Carbury derives from Cairbre, one of Niall's sons.

Carbury COUNTY KILDARE

It is not widely known that the Wellesley family, of which the most famous member was the first Duke of Wellington, used to spell their name Wesley. More importantly, their original name was Colley: in 1728, on inheriting the estates of Dangan and Mornington in County Meath from a cousin, Richard Colley legally adopted the Wesley surname. The grandfather of the Iron Duke, Richard Wesley was eventually created first Baron of Mornington (his son, called Garret Wesley in memory of the man who had bequeathed them his estates, would become first Earl of Mornington in 1760). All this is by way of explaining a link between the Duke of Wellington and Carbury Castle, County Kildare. In the early years of

Elizabeth I's reign, the lands of Carbury were bestowed by the crown on Henry Colley, an English soldier who rose to become an Irish Privy Counsellor and was invested as a Knight in 1574. Several more generations of Colleys followed, until another Henry inherited Carbury in the late seventeenth century: it was his younger son Richard who, when he inherited estates in County Meath, changed his surname to Wesley. The castle, probably dating from the late sixteenth/early seventeenth century, was abandoned in the mid-1700s. A little down the hill from it lies an ancient graveyard, with the remains of a chapel's west gable and the Colley mausoleum, which looks to be of early eighteenth-century origin.

Carstown Manor
COUNTY LOUTH

Inside Carstown Manor, County Louth are a pair of carved limestone plaques, one at the center of a massive chimney piece in what would have been the main reception room, the other directly above the entrance door. Although differing in shape, they carry the same details, namely the date 1612, a coat of arms combining those of two families, and the initials OP and KH. These stand for Oliver Plunkett and his wife Katherine Hussey, who came from Galtrim, County Meath. Both families were long settled in this part of the country and the plaques may be presumed to indicate either the couple's marriage or the date on which they completed work of some kind at Carstown. The year of its original construction is, as so often in Ireland, a matter of conjecture but it was recently proposed that the house's core consists of a late-Medieval house dating from the late fifteenth or early sixteenth century, a rare survivor of domestic architecture from this period. But for how much longer? In 2014 lead was stripped from the roof, along with a set of gates beyond the yard, probably by metal thieves. This exacerbated Carstown's decline as large numbers of slates came free, leaving the floors below exposed to the elements. Then in October 2017, just as some remedial work was about to be undertaken, the house was set on fire and much of its remaining interiors gutted. Carstown's future remains uncertain.

Castle Roche COUNTY LOUTH

Visible high above the fields of County Louth rises a limestone outcrop on which are the remains of a once-substantial fortification. This is Castle Roche, believed to date from the thirteenth century when erected by the Anglo-Norman de Verdun family. An ancestor, Bertram de Verdun had come to England in 1066 as retainer of Count Robert of Mortain, one of William the Conqueror's principal commanders at the Battle of Hastings. His grandson, another Bertram, was appointed seneschal for the visit of Henry II to Ireland in 1171 and granted land in the country. Bertram would die at Jaffa in 1192 while participating in the Third Crusade, but his son Nicholas inherited the Irish estates and married Joan Fitz-Piers, the offspring of another member of the Anglo-Norman settlers. The couple had a daughter, Rohesia de Verdun, and she is traditionally credited with building Castle Roche. She was a considerable heiress, so it is

not surprising that Rohesia should have become linked to another important Anglo-Norman family in Ireland, in 1225 marrying as his second wife Theobold le Boteler, a forebear of the Butler family. Five years later he died during an expedition to Gascony and it was seemingly only after this that she began construction of a mighty fortress on her land: its name, Castle Roche, derives from a corruption of her own, Rohesia. On the other hand, she may not have been directly responsible for the building's erection. However, a persistent legend about Castle Roche proposes that Rohesia declared her intention only to marry the man who could construct a castle to her satisfaction. Someone duly did so, but on their wedding night, as he showed his new bride the spectacular view from a window on the west side, she pushed him through it. Rohesia later retired to a convent she founded in Leicester where she in turn duly died.

Built on the edge of a steep cliff, the plan of Castle Roche is almost triangular, this unusual form being dictated by the nature of the site. Rock formations provide protection to west, north, and south, so that the only access to the building lies on its easterly side.

Louth Hall COUNTY LOUTH

The last Roman Catholic to be executed in England for his faith (although officially it was for high treason), Oliver Plunkett was also the first Irishman to be canonized for some seven centuries when declared a saint in 1975. Born 350 years earlier, Plunkett was a member of a family who traced his origins back to Sir Hugh de Plunkett, a Norman knight who had come to Ireland during the reign of Henry II. His descendants established themselves primarily in Counties Meath and Louth and acquired large land holdings in both. During the Reformation period, they remained loyal to the Catholic religion of their forebears. Oliver Plunkett accordingly became a priest and in 1669 was appointed Archbishop of Armagh. However, hardening government attitudes toward Catholicism following the so-called Popish Plot of 1678 led to his arrest and trial in Dublin the following year. When the authorities in Ireland realized it would be impossible to secure a conviction he was taken to London, found guilty of high treason "for promoting the Roman faith," and hanged, drawn, and quartered at Tyburn in July 1681. One of the buildings associated with Oliver Plunkett is Louth Hall, County Louth: he came to stay here in 1670, provided with lodgings by his namesake and kinsman Oliver Plunkett, sixth Baron Louth. The building, a much-extended late-Medieval tower house, remained with the family until the mid-twentieth century after which it stood empty: at one stage the dining room was used to store bags of grain for a local farmer. Vandals set fire to the already-damaged house in 2000 and left it an almost complete ruin. More recently the Plunkett coat of arms set above the pedimented entrance doorcase was removed, further severing any link with the family.

These pages and overleaf *The core of Louth Hall is a late-Medieval tower house sitting above the river Glyde. Around 1760 a long three-storey, one-room deep extension was added. Additional alterations were made in 1805 when architect Richard Johnston was commissioned to design further spaces, including a ballroom with bow window to the rear of the building.*

Millbrook COUNTY LAOIS

Britain's first purpose-built mosque, the Shah Jahan Mosque in Woking, Surrey has an extraordinary background, being commissioned by a Hungarian-born Jewish linguist, Gottlieb Wilhelm Leitner. Believed to have been familiar with fifty languages, by the age of twenty-three when appointed Professor of Arabic and Muslim Law at King's College, London, Leitner had already acted as translator to the British Commissariat during the Crimean War and traveled throughout the Middle East. In 1864 he became Principal of the newly-established Government College University in Lahore and spent the next couple of decades living and working in what is now India and Pakistan. It was on his return to Britain that Leitner decided to found a center for

the study in Europe of Oriental languages, culture, and history. Coming across a suitable site in Woking, he commissioned the construction of a new mosque in part funded by Shah Jahan, Begum of Bhopal after whom it was named. Opened in 1889, the building was designed by architect William Isaac Chambers who spent the first half of that decade working in Ireland. One of Chambers' last commissions was for this house, Millbrook, County Laois. Built for the agent of the Abbeyleix estate, a scrolled pediment over the doorcase carries the date 1885, just four years before the Shah Jahan Mosque was built in a very different style. But whereas the latter still flourishes, Millbrook has fallen into desuetude.

Palace of Marley COUNTY CARLOW

In Ireland, there are a number of places called Palace or Pallas, which derives from the Norman word *Paleis* meaning boundary fence. Accordingly a house in County Carlow is known as the Palace of Marley (although its other name is Knockduff). A local explanation for why this relatively modest residence should carry the title of palace is that a Roman Catholic bishop was either born or once lived here. An old local rhyme runs as follows:

"Sweet Ballybrack I'll give to Jack,
Inchaphhoka to Charlie,
Ballybeg I'll give to Peg,
And I'll live in the palace of Marley."

Of two storeys and five bays, the building's most immediately striking features are the pediment at the center of the façade and the cut granite used for all the dressings, including door and window cases. As indicated by tall, narrow gable ends, inside the house was just one room deep, there being three on the ground floor and the same number above. The building is officially listed as dating from c.1750 but could be earlier, perhaps 1710–20. Unfortunately, little of the original interior remains other than a rather crude chimney piece and at least some of the old staircase. Some years ago a program of refurbishment was begun but then stopped, leaving the palace in its present unfortunate state.

In the middle of the nineteenth century Piltown was described as "a strikingly beautiful mansion standing in the centre of the (Piltown) townland, within a park of 200 statute acres, that for scenic effect and skilful cultivation, presents, in the view from the Dublin and Drogheda railway, an ornamental and gratifying foreground." Such is no longer the case for either house or surrounding land.

Piltown COUNTY LOUTH

In 1836 Thomas Brodigan, a merchant from Drogheda, County Louth, proposed that a railway line be constructed running along the coast from Dublin to his native town. The local textile industry was in decline and Brodigan believed at least part of the reason for this was poor transport links. A rival scheme was soon devised for the line to run further inland but ultimately Brodigan's plan prevailed and the rail link was duly opened in 1844. Long before this its originator had received a public vote of thanks from the denizens of Drogheda, together with a gold box marking that he had been given the freedom of the town in appreciation of "the zeal and ability which he uniformly evinced in promoting works of public utility..." In the meantime, Brodigan had built a smart new residence

for himself some miles outside Drogheda at Piltown. The house was described in 1844 as "a strikingly beautiful mansion," the design of which was "a compound architecture, presenting a pleasing combination of the Italian with the Grecian style, in which the lightness of the latter prevails." The architect of this handsome Neo-Classical property remains unknown, its most striking interior feature having been a top-lit circular entrance hall with statue niches and panels containing trompe l'oeil paper by the French company of Joseph Dufour et Cie, alas all now gone. In the last century, like so many other such houses, Piltown was acquired and maintained by a religious order, but in more recent decades stood empty until destroyed in 2006 by arsonists.

Duckett's Grove

COUNTY CARLOW

Some buildings make better ruins than do others, but few look as splendid as Duckett's Grove. The remains of this large house rise about the surrounding flat agricultural land, like some nineteenth-century interpretation of a castle in the *Très Riches Heures du Duc de Berry*. Originally at the center of a 12,000-acre estate, the core of the building probably dates from the early 1700s, but from 1818 John Dawson Duckett embarked on a complete transformation of the house, employing the little-known architect Thomas Alfred Cobden. Nothing else the latter designed approaches his work at Duckett's Grove where, presumably at the client's request, he let rip with almost every decorative motif available. The old house was smothered in a superfluity of turrets, crenellations, arches and niches, oriel windows, and quatrefoil decoration before being further embellished with busts and urns and statuary, some of it attached to the building, some free-standing in the immediate grounds. John Dawson Duckett's son William inherited the estate and although twice married, had no children. On his death in 1908 the estate passed to his widow. Eight years later she moved to Dublin and left Duckett's Grove in the hands of an agent. In 1923 the house's contents went in a three-day auction, while the building and remaining land were bought by a group of local farmers. However, they quarrelled over its division and failed to repay the bank, so eventually the Land Commission assumed responsibility and divided up the land between another 48 small holders. Duckett's Grove and its immediate 11 acres were acquired by a Carlow businessman in 1931 for £320. He demolished some of the outbuildings but had yet to decide what to do with the main house when it was mysteriously gutted by fire in April 1933. Today the property is under the care of Carlow County Council.

The design of Duleek House's façade has been attributed to Richard Castle, the most successful and prolific architect in Ireland during the second quarter of the eighteenth century. Born David Riccardo and raised in Dresden, where his father was employed by the Elector of Saxony, Castle had come to Ireland by 1728 and remained here until his death in 1751.

Duleek House COUNTY MEATH

Duleek takes its name from "daimh liag", meaning house of stones. This is probably a reference to the early stone-built church, Saint Cianan's, the remains of which are still visible in the center of the village. But it might also now be applicable to another near-ruin, Duleek House which, while occupied until the start of the present century, has since become threatened with collapse. The building is of interest because its southern side shows how one section was grafted onto another. The date of the earlier portion is unknown, but is probably early eighteenth century. Later Thomas Trotter (died 1745), Member of Parliament for the pocket borough of Duleek, added a new house directly in front of the old. Its design is attributed to the era's most fashionable architect in Ireland, the German-born Richard Castle. Only one room deep, the three-bay front section is faced in crisp limestone ashlar, centered on a tripartite pedimented Doric doorcase with Venetian window directly above. Formerly the interior had handsome Neo-Classical plasterwork in the principal reception rooms and late eighteenth-century joinery. It is impossible to know how much, if any, of this now remains. Or indeed if Duleek House will remain standing for much longer.

These pages and overleaf *This lodge is one of at least six that formerly marked entrances to the Naper estate at Loughcrew. A series of strategic marriages meant that the family at one time owned some 180,000 acres around Ireland. This was the inheritance enjoyed by James Lenox Naper who, despite being stingy to his mistress Julia Johnstone, was believed to have an annual income of more than £20,000.*

Loughcrew COUNTY MEATH

In 1824, the former courtesan Harriette Wilson advised a number of her ex-lovers that in return for a consideration of £200 she would omit their names from a volume of memoirs she was then writing. The Duke of Wellington is famously said to have retorted "Publish and be damned." He duly appeared in the book, as did another Irishman, James Lenox Naper. By the time the work appeared, Naper was a respectably married man living on his estate in County Meath. However, the tale recounted by Wilson concerned Naper's life more than a decade earlier, when he was a young Member of Parliament living in London and conducting a liaison with the author's friend and sister-courtesan Julia Johnstone. The latter was at least fourteen years older than her lover (Harriette Wilson

thought he looked more like her son) and did not find him especially attractive. Nevertheless, she was urged by Wilson to respond to his ardors, not least for the sake of Johnstone's many children: "Napier [sic] is your man," Wilson told her. "Since you could be unchaste to gratify your own passions, I am sure it cannot be wrong to secure the comfort and protection of six beautiful children." Eventually she overcame her reluctance, and while the match was never very happy, it only ended with Johnstone's death in 1815. This delightful rustic lodge in the woods at Loughcrew was commissioned by Naper around 1840 but, like much of the rest of his original estate, has slipped into disrepair.

Oaklands

COUNTY WEXFORD

Originally from Gloucestershire and related to William Tyndale, the sixteenth-century scholar who translated the Bible into English, a branch of the Tyndall family settled in Ireland in the 1650s. At the end of the following decade, the Tyndalls were granted land in County Wexford where they remained for the next 300 years. One of the houses associated with them was Oaklands, situated on raised ground above the River Barrow. The last big house on the site looks to have been built in the early nineteenth century and was of two storeys; its seven-bay façade, with projecting wings on either side, was centered on a long pillared portico constructed of local granite. The last of the family to live here died in 1957, shortly after which the building was destroyed by fire. Today just the portico stands, although the surrounding grounds are littered with cut stone from the now-lost house: a bungalow has been built where it once stood.

Rosmead

COUNTY WESTMEATH

This triumphal arch marks the entrance to Rosmead, County Westmeath. Its design attributed to English architect Samuel Woolley (his only work in Ireland) and dating from the mid-1790s, the arch is of limestone embellished with Coade stone ornamentation. Now badly weathered, the design once also included urns and statuary, but this has all long-since gone. The arch was originally erected at Glananea some seven miles away in the same county. The latter property had been built in 1784 by Ralph Smyth, whose family owned several estates in the area and who called his property Ralphsdale. Having had the arch erected, he came to be known locally as "Smyth with the Gates." This nickname appears to have remained in circulation for many decades but eventually in the middle of the nineteenth century Ralph Smyth disposed of the arch to its present home. It seems that thereafter the family were given the new nomenclature of "Smyth without the Gates." Ironically Rosmead—once a fine seven-bay country house—fell into dereliction in the 1940s and is now just a shell, while Glananea still stands. Perhaps it would have been better for the arch to have remained in its original setting.

Lower Crossdrum COUNTY MEATH

In February 1840 Charles Cockerell wrote from England to fellow architect Richard Morrison, who had invited the former to become an honorary member of the newly-formed Institute of Architects of Ireland. In the latter country, Cockerell remarked, "I have experienced some of the most delightful hours of my Art, in modern works as well especially of those of the middle of the last century… I have traced your own works with the greatest pleasure, tho' never so fortunate as to meet you. I retain the most agreeable remembrance of your beautiful Country and Metroplis and wish I could often see them, but the distance and a family and occupations here preclude it." Cockerell had paid a couple of visits to Ireland in the 1820s when overseeing the construction of Loughcrew

(see page 41), a vast classical house which, having suffered fire three times in the course of 100 years, was eventually demolished in the 1960s. Cockerell managed to fit in a number of other commissions during his Irish trips when he stayed with the agent of the Loughcrew estate, Edward Rotherham, who gradually built up his own quite substantial estate. Rotherham's former residence, seen here, dates from around the time of his marriage in 1822. Its ashlar limestone façade is centered on a Tuscan porch with tripartite doorcase behind and fanlight above. Inside, there was once good plasterwork attributed to George Stapleton. Little evidence of what Cockerell saw when staying here remains, Lower Crossdrum having fallen into ruin in recent decades.

The plasterwork that once adorned Lower Crossdrum is believed to have been designed by George Stapleton, son of the famous stuccodore Michael Stapleton. Examples of the younger man's work survive in Dublin Castle and the adjacent Chapel Royal, among other places.

Donore COUNTY WESTMEATH

For hundreds of years Donore was occupied by a branch of the Nugent family, the first of whom, Hugh de Nugent, came to Ireland in the twelfth century and received lands in Westmeath. In the fifteenth century one of his descendants, James Nugent, married the heiress Elizabeth Holywood and it appears that through her inheritance the lands of Donore passed to the couple's descendants. In the seventeenth century, the Nugents of Donore fought with their Irish compatriots in the Confederate Wars and were duly indicted: despite consistently remaining Roman Catholic, somehow they managed to retain their property. In fact, by judicious marriages they improved their circumstances. In the eighteenth century, for example, James Nugent, first baronet, married Catherine King, elder daughter and co-heiress of Robert King of Drewstown, County Meath. And so it continued into the middle of the last century when, shortly before her death in November 1957, the widowed Aileen, Lady Nugent sold the estate to the Franciscan order which had re-settled nearby on land gifted to the friars by the Nugents. According to the present head of the family, the price paid for this transaction was £20,000. Apparently Lady Nugent had insisted as a condition of the sale that the house would be preserved. However this was not to be. The Franciscans subsequently sold on the greater part of the estate to the Land Commission, Donore was duly condemned, and pulled down. Today a bungalow occupies the site and the estate's splendid eighteenth-century stableyard has fallen into ruin.

Following its acquisition in the eighteenth century by the Tyrrells, a single-storey extension was added to Grange Castle. A finely carved limestone doorcase has a pediment containing the family coat of arms and their motto Veritas Via Vitae *(a variant of Christ's words in St John's Gospel, "I am the way, the truth, and the life").*

Grange Castle COUNTY KILDARE

Set in the midst of a series of stone enclosures, Grange Castle is most likely a fifteenth-century tower house, one of a number of defensive properties built by the Bermingham family in this part of the country. At some date in the late sixteenth/early seventeenth century it was modernized, as can be seen by the larger window openings, the tall chimney stacks (indicating an increased number of hearths), and the ornamental crenellations around the roofline. Further improvements appear to have occurred some time after 1735, when Walter Bermingham sold Grange Castle to Thomas Tyrrell. Subsequently a single-storey house was added to the immediate west. Linked to the castle at the rear, this evidently contained the main reception rooms, with the older section presumably being utilized as sleeping quarters. The main point of access was through the house, via a fine carved limestone doorcase. Grange Castle remained in the ownership of the Tyrrells until 1988 when responsibility for the Medieval structure was handed over to the state. In the mid-1990s a private charitable trust was established to restore the property with the intention of opening it to the public. Over the course of several years a considerable amount of work was undertaken to improve both house and grounds. However, in 2003 this enterprise came to a close and the place has since sat empty.

Kilmacurragh COUNTY WICKLOW

Surrounded by superlative gardens developed between the seventeenth and nineteenth centuries, Kilmacurragh is located on the site of an early Christian settlement established by Saint Mochorog, said to be an Englishman of royal birth who came to Ireland in the early 600s. In 1697 Thomas Acton secured a lease on the property from the Parsons family, then as now based in Birr, County Offaly (where their gardens are likewise renowned). From their moment of arrival at Kilmacurragh, the Actons were keenly interested in the improvement of their demesne. Presumably around the same period that he built the present house at the close of the seventeenth century, Thomas laid out a formal Dutch-style park, with canals and avenues. He also created a 40-acre Deer Park. In turn, his son William Acton laid out a two-mile beech avenue to celebrate his marriage to Jane Parsons in 1736. From the 1850s onward, another Thomas Acton and his sister Janet worked closely with David Moore, then curator of the Botanic Gardens at Glasnevin, Dublin, and later with his son and successor in the position, Sir Frederick Moore. During this period Kilmacurragh became an unofficial outpost for the Botanic Gardens and in recent decades its grounds have been admirably managed by that institution. Sadly the house, which is important as an early example of an unfortified private residence and was likely designed by Sir William Robinson, Ireland's Surveyor General in the later seventeenth century, has fared less well. Following two fires in 1978 and 1982 the building is in urgent need of salvation before what remains is forever lost.

Extant photographs of Kilmacurragh's interior show that when still intact the center portion contained a paneled hall with a staircase featuring barley-sugar balusters. The wings on either side of the main block were added in the 1840s by Lt Col. William Acton.

The last direct descendant of Stephenstown's original builder was Matthew Fortescue who in 1894 married a cousin, Edith Fairlie-Cuninghame. He died twenty years later without a direct heir, after which his widow married an Australian clergyman, the Rev. Henry Pyke, who took on the Fortescue surname to become Pyke-Fortescue. Following the couple's deaths, the house passed to another relative but has stood empty and ever more derelict since the 1970s.

Stephenstown COUNTY LOUTH

During the reign of James I, the splendidly-named Sir Faithful Fortescue, whose family originated in Devon, moved to Ireland where he bought an estate in County Louth. From him descended several branches of the Fortescues, one of whom eventually acquired the titles of Viscount and Earl of Clermont. Meanwhile, the parcel of land first acquired by Sir Faithful was further supplemented by various successors and came to include an estate called Stephenstown. Here sometime around 1785–90, Matthew Fortescue built a new house to mark his marriage to Mary-Anne McClintock. This was a large square building of two storeys over raised basement and with five bays to each side. Around 1820, the next generation of Fortescues added single-storey over-basement wings on either side, but that to the

south was subsequently demolished. Scant remnants indicate the interior had delicate Neo-Classical plasterwork, perhaps on the ceilings (none of which survive) and certainly on friezes below the cornice in diverse rooms. The last direct descendant of the original builder was another Matthew Fortescue who in 1894 married a cousin, Edith Fairlie-Cuninghame. The couple had no children and after passing through a couple of other hands, Stephenstown was left to stand empty. When Alistair Rowan and Christine Casey published a volume on the *Buildings of North Leinster* in 1993, they noted that Stephenstown was "an elegant house, too large for modern rural life, empty in 1985, and likely to become derelict." That likelihood has since become a reality.

Dunmoe Castle

COUNTY MEATH

Sitting high on a bluff above the Boyne, Dunmoe Castle presents a near-blank wall flanked by circular towers. Seen from the river bank below, it is easy to imagine the rest of the building being equally substantial. However, despite putting on a good front, Dunmoe is the Potemkin village of Irish castles: nothing lies behind its fine façade. It is believed the original structure here was built in the twelfth century by the Anglo-Norman knight Hugh de Lacy. By the mid-fifteenth century the lands on which it stands had passed into the hands of another family of Norman origin, the d'Arcys. Inevitably they were caught up in the troubles of the Confederate Wars, Dunmoe being taken by the Irish forces in 1641 and later fired at across the Boyne by the passing Cromwellian Army. Following the restoration of Charles II, in 1663 Thomas d'Arcy was declared "an innocent Papist." It was he who is said to have entertained James II at Dunmoe on the night before the Battle of the Boyne in July 1690, and the victorious William III on the night after. This is supposed to have inspired the couplet, "Who will be king, I do not know/But I'll be d'Arcy of Dunmoe." Indeed the d'Arcys remained at Dunmoe for much of the eighteenth century, converting what had been a fortress into a more comfortable house. The last of them to occupy it appears to have been Judge d'Arcy. Dying young in 1766, he left an infant heiress Elizabeth who would later marry Major Gorges Irvine of Castle Irvine, County Fermanagh (see page 149s). Dunmoe survived until the end of the century before being largely destroyed by fire during the 1798 rebellion.

Tower houses were never particularly luxurious. In 1588, for example, the Spaniard Francisco de Cuéllar wrote "The Irish have no furniture and sleep on the ground, on a bed of rushes, wet with rain and stiff with frost..."

Kilbline Castle COUNTY KILKENNY

Around 1735 Daniel and Hannah Candler left County Kilkenny and emigrated to the America Colonies, initially settling in North Carolina before they moved to Bedford, Virginia. Their great, great, great-grandson was Asa Griggs Candler, an entrepreneur who in 1888 bought the formula for Coca Cola and made himself fabulously rich as a result. His forebear William Candler, originally from Newcastle in Northumberland, is believed to have served as an officer in Oliver Cromwell's army during the Irish wars of 1649–53. As a reward for his endeavor, he was promoted to the rank of Lieutenant Colonel and granted lands in County Kilkenny, including those on which stands Kilbline Castle. In many respects this is a typical Irish tower house. Rising five storeys high, it has round bartizans or wall-mounted turrets at each corner of the east front and a slender chimney-stack between them.

The surrounding bawn wall survives in part but some sections were demolished in the last century to permit the erection of modern farm sheds. Kilbline is usually dated to the fourteenth and fifteenth centuries, but a large limestone chimneypiece on the first floor carries the date 1580, so it is possible that was the year the building was completed. On the other hand, there is reference to Kilbline Castle being forfeited by one Thomas Comerford in 1566, so perhaps the chimneypiece was inserted into the tower by a subsequent owner. As so often, we will likely never know. Kilbline Castle continued to be occupied until just a few decades ago. At some point, probably in the nineteenth century, a two storey three-bay house was added on the west end of the tower house and a further single-storey structure abuts this. All now stand empty.

CHAPTER 2

MUNSTER

Covering the south/south-west of Ireland, Munster derives its name from the Gaelic word *Mumhan* and the Old Norse *staðr*, meaning "The Land of Mumha," the latter being a Pagan goddess. The province includes six counties: Clare, Cork, Kerry, Limerick, Tipperary, and Waterford. For a period during the early Middle Ages, the greater part of Munster was under the control of the Eóganachta dynasty centered on Cashel, County Tipperary. However, by the twelfth century, it had fractured into three kingdoms, the largest of which was that of Desmond, ruled by the MacCarthy family. The kingdom of Thomond, which largely corresponds to present-day counties Limerick and Clare, was ruled by the O'Briens and the smaller and weaker kingdom of Ormond by the O'Kennedys. The three crowns on the flag of Munster represent these three kingdoms, which experienced further encroachment with the arrival of Anglo-Norman families such as the Butlers and FitzGeralds who carved out large territories for themselves.

Glenbeigh Towers is sometimes known as Winn's Folly and it is easy to understand why: funded by ever-increasing rents imposed on Allanson-Winn's tenants, the house suffered from such excessive damp that it proved uninhabitable.

Glenbeigh Towers COUNTY KERRY

Glenbeigh Towers was built between 1867 and 1871 for the Hon. Rowland Allanson-Winn, its design by English architect Edward Godwin. The latter's only other Irish commission was Dromore, County Limerick (see page 74) but both properties proved to suffer from the same problems: the budget overran and the walls perpetually leaked. Whereas Godwin's patron at Dromore, the third Earl of Limerick, stoically suffered these inconveniences, Allanson-Winn was not prepared to do so and sued his architect for the cost of employing someone else to rectify the issue. Godwin settled the case before it came to court but thereafter would advise, "When offered a commission in Ireland, refuse it." Glenbeigh was only ever occupied

by staff until taken over by members of the British Military Command during the First World War. It was subsequently burnt by the Irish Republican Army in 1921 and has remained a striking ruin ever since. Incidentally Allanson-Winn's son, Rowland George Allanson-Winn, became fifth Lord Headley following the death of a cousin in January 1913: eight months later he converted to Islam and made a pilgrimage to Mecca the following decade (after which he was known as Al-Haj Shaikh Saifurrahman Rehmatullah El-Farooq). A champion boxer in his youth, he is also remembered for having been offered the throne of Albania twice… and refusing on both occasions.

During the years of the Great Famine (1845-48) Arthur Kiely-Ussher did not reduce or suspend his hard-pressed tenants' rents, as did others in his position around the country, but used non-payment as a justification for eviction and the demolition of any dwelling. There was therefore little regret when soon afterward he was forced to sell the Ballysaggartmore estate.

Ballysaggartmore Towers COUNTY WATERFORD

In the second decade of the nineteenth century, Arthur Kiely built a comfortable and unassuming residence at Ballysaggartmore. But in the 1830s, following his marriage to Elizabeth Martin of Ross House, County Galway (a great-aunt of Violet Martin, one half of the writing duo Somerville and Ross), he not only changed his surname to Kiely-Ussher but embarked on an ambitious building program on his estate. Ultimately ambition outstripped resources and only an elaborate gate lodge and bridge flanked by a pair of miniature castles were completed before the onset of the Great Famine. Short of funds, Kiely-Ussher displayed so little concern for his starving tenants that at least one attempt was made to murder him. In the aftermath of this catastrophe, he was left penniless and forced to sell Ballysaggartmore. At the

start of the last century, the estate was bought the Hon Claud Anson following his marriage to Lady Clodagh de la Poer Beresford, daughter of the fifth Marquess of Waterford. However, the couple did not enjoy the place for long as in 1922 Ballysaggartmore House was destroyed by fire. In any case, by then the Ansons' funds had—like those of Arthur Kiely-Ussher before them—run out; according to Patrick Cockburn (a godson of their daughter) this was owing to "Claud's overenthusiastic investment in Russian bonds prior to the Revolution." The house stood empty and derelict until pulled down some decades later. The front lodges, however, remained occupied until the 1970s, after which they, too, were abandoned and allowed to fall into ruin.

Buttevant Castle <small>COUNTY CORK</small>

Of Norman origin, the Barrys were one of the dominant families of Munster, created Barons Barry in the mid-thirteenth century, then Viscounts Buttevant in 1541 and finally Earls of Barrymore in 1627. The last holders of the title, together with their siblings, became famous in late eighteenth-century London for their unruly behavior. Richard, the seventh earl, a close friend of the Prince of Wales, was a notorious rake, gambler, and bare-knuckle boxer. His wild ways earned him the name Hellgate, while his younger brother Henry, who inherited the title after Richard died at the age of 23, had a clubfoot and was accordingly nicknamed Cripplegate. Meanwhile the third sibling, Augustus, despite being an Anglican clergyman, became so addicted to gambling that he was known as Newgate, supposedly because this was the only debtors' prison in which he had not spent time. Finally, the brothers' only sister, Lady Caroline Barry swore with such frequency and proficiency that she was called Billingsgate, after the foul-tongued fishwives of that market. Between them, the four managed to dissipate

their once-great estates in Ireland, including extensive lands surrounding Buttevant Castle, which had been held by the Barrys since the early 1200s. Dating back to the thirteenth century, the building was bought by John Anderson and given its present external appearance around 1810. Occupied until the start of the last century, it has since fallen into ruin.

After some six centuries of ownership, the Barrys were forced to sell Buttevant Castle to John Anderson, a Scottish entrepreneur who moved to County Cork around 1780 and developed the town of Fermoy. It was he who gave the building its present castellated appearance.

These pages and overleaf *No expense was spared in the construction of Dromdiah: an account written in the 1860s noted that the house "consists of a centre and two wings, ornamented with Doric columns and with a portico at the eastern end, by which the hall is entered, and off which are hot, cold, vapour and shower baths."*

Dromdiah COUNTY CORK

Dromdiah, sometimes called Dromdihy, suggests it is never a good idea for a landowner to neglect his property. The house was built c.1833 by Roger Green Davis who acted as land agent for Sir Arthur de Capell-Brooke, an absentee landlord. Sir Arthur was an explorer who traveled through Scandinavia and published several books about what he had seen. When not engaged in these activities, he lived in Northamptonshire, hence the need for someone to look after his Irish estate. One wonders how much attention Sir Arthur ever paid to it since Roger Green Davis was able to build up a landholding of more than 2,250 acres in County Cork, albeit some of it rented from the de Capell-Brooke estate. And on his own land he decided to build a house

proclaiming his new status. Dromdiah's architectural style is so pared back, so devoid of extraneous ornament, so uncompromisingly faithful to the ideology of Greek Revivalism it might have come from the hand of a Schinkel or von Klenze. But if the design was admirable, its execution left something to be desired: seemingly from the start the house suffered from damp, the roof leaking, and the interior manifesting both dry and wet rot. Understandably, it changed hands a number of times until the mid-1940s when deemed uninhabitable and unroofed. Dromdiah looked set to remain a striking ruin but the house has recently been bought, its new owners ambitiously planning to restore the building as a private residence.

Dromore Castle COUNTY LIMERICK

Driving west from Limerick city, the eye is caught by immense battlemented ruins on the horizon. These are the remains of Dromore Castle, built 150 years ago and unroofed for the past sixty. Situated on a promontory overlooking a lake and with sweeping views across the Shannon estuary, Dromore's dramatic silhouette, as has often been observed, would not look out of place above the Rhine. Yet one of the paradoxes of this extravagant building is that the architect responsible was anxious it be historically accurate to Ireland. Dromore was designed in 1866 by Edward William Godwin, his client being William Pery, third Earl of Limerick. On receiving the commission, Godwin went to a great deal of trouble to make sure the castle was authentically Irish in design. With his friend and fellow architect William Burges (then working on Saint Fin Barre's Cathedral in Cork) he travelled around the country drawing and measuring old castles and churches; what he saw during the journey influenced the eventual building, finished by 1869. Intended to emulate a Medieval castle, Dromore incorporates a round tower, something not as a rule found in domestic residences, but Godwin included it on the grounds that such towers were found on fortified sites like that at the Rock of Cashel. When the place was finished Lord Limerick professed himself "extremely delighted" with the result, but neither he nor his successors spent much time there, perhaps because the castle was extremely uncomfortable and permanently damp. Sold at the end of the 1930s, it was unroofed twenty years later to avoid the payment of rates, a common fate for old houses at the time. So Dromore Castle has remained ever since, indomitable as Godwin intended and proving able to withstand the assault of time and an inclement climate.

These pages and overleaf

Every element of Dromore Castle's decoration — furnishings, wall paintings, chimneypieces, stained glass, tiles, brass- and ironwork — was overseen by the building's architect William Godwin. Indeed, it appears he even chose the location, scouring his client's land until he found "a dream-like situation on the edge of a wood… overlooking the water, which would reflect the castle one hundred feet below."

Dunlough Castle COUNTY CORK

A thousand years ago the O'Mahonys were a powerful family occupying territory in Munster, running from where Cork city now stands to the south-west of the region. However, following the Norman invasion in the second half of the twelfth century, the O'Mahonys were gradually pushed ever closer to the Atlantic, ultimately settling on a number of peninsulas jutting into the ocean. Here, according to the Medieval *Annals of Inisfallen*, they built themselves a fortified settlement in a place now known as Dunlough Castle. It is easy to understand why the location was chosen. To the east lies a lake, Dun Lough, which would have provided fish for the building's occupants. To north and south the land rises steeply, making it possible to anticipate potential attack, since anyone intending to do so would have been visible on the horizon. Meanwhile, immediately to the west are cliffs dropping precipitately to the Atlantic. What remains today is a fifteenth-century development of the site. This gives Dunlough its popular name of Three Castles since the structure comprises a trio of fortified towers joined by a wall some 20 feet high and almost 1,000 feet long running from cliff to lakeshore. The O'Mahonys remained here until the 1620s when their lands were confiscated. The last occupants are believed to have been members of the O'Donohue family, all of whom apparently died by murder or suicide: according to legend, a drop of blood falls every day in the tower closest to the lake.

All three of Dunlough Castle's towers are rectangular and three storeys high, the most substantial being that furthest to the west. Rising almost 50 feet and over 50 square feet inside, the building would have been used to provide the castle's main accommodation.

Kanturk Castle COUNTY CORK

On a map of Ireland made by John Norden between 1609 and 1611, there is a castle shown at "Cantork" (Kanturk). It would appear this had been constructed not long before, probably by Dermot MacCormac MacCarthy, Lord of Duhallow. The castle is rectangular, measuring 92 by 36 feet and rising four storeys with a five-storey, 95 foot high tower at each corner. The main entrance is on the western side, a work of Italian Renaissance inspiration with an elaborate entablature above Ionic columns on either side of a round-headed doorframe. Seemingly in order to pay for the building's construction, MacCormac MacCarthy mortgaged large tracts of his territory even though under Gaelic law all such land was deemed communal property. The mortgagee was Sir Philip Perceval, forebear of the Earls of Egmont, who had arrived in Ireland in 1579 and by such means was able

to amass a large estate for himself. No documentation survives about Kanturk Castle's construction, but one legend claims it was built by seven stone-masons, all named John: for a time the building was known as "Carrig-na-Shane-Saor" (the Rock of John the Mason). Work on the site seems to have stopped in 1618 after English settlers in the area objected to the castle being too large and too fortified. Accordingly the English Privy Council ordered that work be discontinued. It is said that MacCormac MacCarthy was so angry at this instruction that he ordered the blue ceramic tiles on the castle's roof be smashed and thrown into a nearby stream, which thereafter was known as Bluepool. Likewise, according to popular belief, following his fit of pique over the Privy Council order, MacCormac MacCarthy never occupied Kanturk Castle but left it the shell seen today.

Kilmanahan Castle COUNTY WATERFORD

Perched high over the Suir river, Kilmanahan Castle, County Waterford, has at its core a Medieval castle erected by the FitzGeralds. In 1586 the land on which it stood was acquired (as part of a parcel of some 11,500 acres) by Sir Edward Fitton, whose father had come to this country from England and risen to be Lord President of Connaught and Vice-Treasurer of Ireland. However, Fitton seems to have over-extended himself and this may explain why in the early years of the seventeenth century Kilmanahan was bought by Sir James Gough, whose family were wealthy merchants in Waterford city. The castle next changed hands in 1678 when granted to Godfrey Greene, son of another English-born planter. A captain in what was called the King's Irish Protestant Army, Greene had remained loyal to the crown during the Cromwellian interregnum and thus benefited from the return of the monarchy in 1660. His descendants gradually enlarged Kilmanahan and remained in residence until the mid-nineteenth century when forced to sell the estate through the Encumbered Estates' Court. After changing hands a couple more times, at the start of the last century the property was bought by the Hely-Hutchinsons, Earls of Donoughmore, whose main estate, Knocklofty, lay on the other side of the Suir. The Donoughmores sold up and left Ireland more than thirty years ago, but even by then the building had fallen on hard times: an American visitor in the mid-1980s remembers exploring the site and seeing cattle occupying the former reception rooms.

Although the core of Kilmanahan Castle is a Medieval castle, much of its present appearance dates from the late eighteenth/ early nineteenth centuries when greatly extended by Lieutenant-Colonel Nuttall Greene and his wife Charlotte Ann Parsons, perhaps to accommodate their large family (they had five sons and nine daughters).

The great Ionic portico that still dominates the façade of Mount Shannon was added to the house by the second Earl of Clare in the early nineteenth century, the architect responsible being Lewis Wyatt, a nephew and pupil of James Wyatt.

Mount Shannon COUNTY LIMERICK

Many stories are told of John "Black Jack" Fitzgibbon, first Earl of Clare, some of them probably apocryphal, none of them kind. After studying at Trinity College, Dublin and Christ Church, Oxford, he became a lawyer and was elected to the Irish House of Commons in 1778. Five years later he became Attorney General for Ireland, then Lord Chancellor in 1789. Created a Viscount in 1793, he received his earldom in 1795. Unquestionably brilliant, Fitzgibbon was also undoubtedly bigoted. He supported harsh measures against supporters of the 1798 Rebellion and was hostile to Roman Catholicism despite—or perhaps because of—his father having originally been a member of this faith. When it came to the Act of Union in 1800, of which he was firmly in favor, there was widespread understanding that this would be accompanied by concessions made to Roman Catholics

through amelioration of the Penal Laws: Fitzgibbon persuaded George III that any such liberalization of the status quo would be a violation of the King's Coronation Oath and thus ensured pro-Emancipation measures were not included in the Union legislation. Supposedly Fitzgibbon once declared he would make his fellow countrymen as "tame as a dead cat." As a result, there are stories of dead cats being thrown into his coach, and of more of the same being flung into his grave when he died in 1802 following a fall from his horse at Mount Shannon the previous month. The house, bought by his father and aggrandized by his son, had to be sold in the late 1880s following the bankruptcy of his granddaughter. Mount Shannon then passed through several hands before being burnt in June 1920, the light of the flames apparently seen in Limerick city several miles away.

In 1839 Lady Chatterton recorded that almost two centuries earlier, Leamaneh Castle's most famous occupant, Máire ní Mahon, on hearing her first husband Conor O'Brien had been killed by an English soldier, captured and hanged the man responsible before marrying one of his fellow officers to secure her son's inheritance.

Leamaneh Castle COUNTY CLARE

Leamaneh Castle originally consisted of a plain five-storey tower house (the section to the right of the building). This was constructed around 1480 by Turlogh O'Brien, King of Thomond, and is said to derive its name from the Irish "Leim an eich" (The Horse's Leap). In 1543, Turlogh O'Brien's son, Murrough, surrendered the castle and pledged loyalty to the English crown; as a result he was duly created first Earl of Thomond and Baron Inchiquin. In 1648, his descendant Conor O'Brien extended the tower with the addition of a four-storey manor house following his marriage to Máire ní Mahon who, on account of her flaming red hair, was commonly known as Máire Rúa (Red Mary). Many legends are told of Máire Rúa, most of them apocryphal (such as that which proposes she had 25 husbands, after which she was sealed into a hollow tree

and left to die). However, it is true that after Conor O'Brien was killed by an English soldier, she married a Cromwellian officer, thereby ensuring the family estates were preserved for her son, Sir Donough O'Brien. He was the last of the family to reside at Leamaneh, moving instead to live at the larger and more commodious Dromoland Castle. Early in the last century Sir Donough's descendant, Lucius William O'Brien, 15th Baron Inchiquin organized for a stone gateway hitherto marking the entrance to Leamaneh to be removed and re-erected in the grounds of Dromoland, where it still remains. Around the same time a stone chimneypiece from the castle was also taken out and installed in the Old Ground Hotel, Ennis, where it can be seen today.

Kilballyowen COUNTY LIMERICK

In 1968, the big house at Kilballyowen, County Limerick, was demolished. Its then-owner, Lieutenant Colonel Gerald Vigors de Courcy O'Grady—whose family have been based there for hundreds of years—later recalled, "The huge rooms were too big to live in; it was impossible to live in a house of that nature. If you could live there in warm conditions—yes. It was just a necessity. No, I didn't just want to leave it empty, so there are no remains. I do not like living near ruins; there are too many around here." His wife commented that by the late 1960s the house "was in a terrifying state of repair and we did not have the money to fix it. We had thought of selling just the house, but then we were afraid we might lose the land as well. It was a great house that had lost its pride." There was no support for the owners and no state interest in the preservation of such properties. And so, like very many others, Kilballyowen came down. The core of the building had been a tower house dating from c.1500, around which a modern residence had been constructed in the first half of the eighteenth century and then further extended by a new wing in 1810. In 1837, Samuel Lewis described the property as "a handsome modern building in a richly planted demesne." Kilballyowen had a five-bay facade with a two-bay projecting extension to one side: the garden front featured a three-bay breakfront. While nothing of the house remains, the stableyard to the immediate north-west just about survives as testimony to what has been lost.

These pages and overleaf *The core of the now-demolished Kilballyowen was a tower house dating from c.1500, around which a house had been built in the first half of the eighteenth century, and then further extended by a new wing in 1810: in 1837 Samuel Lewis described the property as "a handsome modern building in a richly planted demesne."*

In the first half of the eighteenth century John Perceval lavished attention on Lohort Castle, laying out formal classical gardens with long straight vistas and canals, while alterations made inside the building included the provision of a library and a well-stocked armory.

Lohort Castle COUNTY CORK

As so often in Ireland, Lohort Castle's origins are uncertain. It has been proposed a castle was constructed here in the late twelfth century on the instructions of Prince (future King) John, but more likely this was another of the innumerable tower houses that appeared on the Irish landscape in the fifteenth and sixteenth centuries. As such, it would have been built for the MacCarthys, who were then the dominant family in the region. At the time, the castle would have been at the center of a larger site with other buildings surrounded by an enclosing wall. In plan and form, it is typical of the Irish tower house, being rectangular and rising five storeys to a machicolated parapet (openings through which hot oil or other substances could be dropped onto attackers), with only one small point of access on the ground floor. The

building's most striking feature is its curved external walls, which, while unusual, are not unique. An engraving from the early 1740s shows it looking much as is still the case today, albeit surrounded by a moat (drained in 1876) and protected by star-shaped outerworks in the style of those developed by the Marquis de Vauban, a seventeenth-century French military engineer. At the time of this work the castle's owner was John Perceval, created first Earl of Egmont in 1733. The only obvious differences are the stepped gable on the east side of the roof and the chimney stacks: these were added toward the end of the nineteenth century. The building was burnt by the IRA in July 1921 but was sufficiently sturdy to survive and, after some restoration work, to be habitable once more. This no longer looks to be the case.

At the time of its construction in the 1630s the design of Mount Long Castle would have embodied contemporary architectural fashion in Ireland. By this date domestic dwellings were no longer being built as tower houses but, in misplaced expectation of future peace, as fortified manor houses. Within a decade, Ireland was at war, and Mount Long Castle at risk.

Mount Long Castle COUNTY CORK

Once prominent in the East Muskerry region of County Cork, the Long family is believed to be descended from a branch of the Ui Eachach. By the late Medieval period, their base was at Canovee, otherwise called Cannaway, and often referred to as an island since so much of the area is surrounded by water, with the river Lee to the immediate north, north-east, and north-west, the river Kame and one of its tributaries to the east, and another stream to the west. The Civil Survey of the Barony of Muskerry conducted in 1656 lists a great deal of the land around here as having belonged to "John Long of Mount Long, Irish Papist (deceased)." This John Long was the son of Dr Thomas Long, a doctor of civil and canon law who had evidently prospered since he was able

to acquire land elsewhere in County Cork, specifically to the south overlooking Oysterhaven Creek. Here in 1631 John Long embarked on building himself a new residence, named Mount Long. He did not occupy it for long. A decade later began the conflict known as the Confederate Wars in which Long and his two sons took the side of the Roman Catholic forces. Defeated close to Bandon, Long was taken prisoner, convicted of treason, and hanged. It is said that knowing his fate, he sent a message to his daughter at Mount Long in 1643, telling her to burn the house in order to stop it falling into enemy hands. Whether true or not, the building was certainly consumed by fire at some date: still extant lintels over doors and windows show evidence of scorch marks.

Ardtully COUNTY KERRY

Like many families, the Orpens were inclined to claim a more distinguished pedigree than was actually merited. So in *Burke's Landed Gentry* of 1847 it was asserted "The family of Orpen is of remote antiquity, and is stated to trace its descent from Erpen, second son of Varnacker (maire of the palace to Clothaire I), who was the son of Meroveus, and grandson of Theodorick, son of Clovis, King of France." This places the Orpens' origins back in the sixth century and, by the time he won the Battle of Hastings in 1066, William of Normandy was of course accompanied by a knight called Robert d'Erpen, who supposedly settled at Erpingham in Norfolk. According to this version of events, the family turned up in Ireland in the second half of the seventeenth century as members of the landed gentry on the other side of the Irish Sea. However, the year before his death in 1932, the historian Goddard Henry Orpen produced an alternative and somewhat less distinguished narrative. From this it

would appear that the first Orpen to come to Ireland, a descendant of humble yeomen stock, did so some time in the 1650s or 1660s. Twenty years later his son, Richard Orpen was employed as a land agent by the region's greatest landowner, Sir William Petty. All of which is not quite as splendid as the lineage proposed by Burke but, as Goddard Henry Orpen wrote, "it is the truth I seek and not a (faked) illustrious ancestry and, after all, is it not better to rise than to fall?" And after all, the Orpens did rise so that by the time *Burke's Landed Gentry* was published, they had embarked on building this fine residence for themselves at Ardtully, County Kerry. It remained their home until burnt by the IRA in 1921.

By the nineteenth century, the Orpens had built up a land holding of more than 12,000 acres and needed a residence to reflect their status. Dating from the late 1840s, Ardtully is a typical Victorian grab-bag of architectural elements, its most prominent feature being a castellated round tower and turret on the south-east corner.

*Otherwise known
as Everard's Castle,
Burncourt is a substantial
four-bay, three-storey over
basement rectangular
block with square flanking
towers of four storeys at
each corner. The building
is notable for its gables,
all 26 of them, and when
constructed it had seven
chimney stacks.*

Burncourt COUNTY TIPPERARY

In 1613 the only Irish Parliament held during the reign of James I was called, to which Sir John Everard was returned as member of the House of Commons for Tipperary. He was the Roman Catholic members' choice for the position of Speaker of the House, but Catholics were in a minority, the government's man being Sir John Davies, Attorney General for Ireland. When the vote was taken, Everard installed himself in the Speaker's chair and refused to budge. According to a contemporary source, "Sir Thomas Ridgway, Sir Richard Wingfield, Sir Oliver St John and others, brought Sir John Davies to the chair, and lifted him into Sir John Everard's lap; the Knights perceiving Sir John Everard would not give place to their speaker, they lifted Sir John Everard out of the chair, and some of Sir John Everard's part holding him by the collar of the gown to keep him in the chair…"

Ultimately this undignified incident ended in Everard's defeat, not least because Sir John Davies was a much heavier man who literally crushed his opponent by sitting on top of him. If only that farcical episode was the worst fate to befall the family. In the late 1630s Sir John's son, Sir Richard Everard, embarked on building a fashionable residence for himself on his estate in County Tipperary. Soon afterward he became embroiled in the Confederate Wars and, following capture after the Siege of Limerick, was hanged by General Ireton in 1651. The year before, as Cromwell's army advanced south, rather than let the family's fine new house fall into enemy hands, Lady Everard set the place on fire: it has stood a ruin ever since, and is known as Burncourt. According to legend, the building took seven years to build, was occupied for seven years, and burned for seven days.

Kilcooley COUNTY TIPPERARY

"Therefore his servants said to him, 'Let a young woman be sought for my lord the king, and let her wait on the king and be in his service. Let her lie in your arms, that my lord the king may be warm'." (1 Kings 1:2). William Ponsonby-Barker of Kilcooley, County Tipperary, was an ardent evangelical Christian. In the years prior to his death in 1877, he would habitually emulate the example of King David in the Old Testament by taking a young woman to bed with him—strictly for the purposes of keeping his elderly body warm. The human hot water bottle would, it is said, be chosen from among the housemaids lined up after evening prayers. Seemingly on one occasion the maid's smell was not to Ponsonby-Barker's liking, so he doused her with what in the darkness he took to be a bottle of eau de Cologne: it turned out to be ink. Begun in the 1760s and overlooking the remains of a former Cistercian monastery, Kilcooley's interiors date from the early 1840s after a butler, dismissed by Ponsonby-Barker for fathering a child out of wedlock with a local woman, took his revenge by stuffing the library chimney with paper and setting it alight. As a result, the building was gutted. During the subsequent renovation, an immense double-height entrance hall was created with first-floor gallery, the whole lit by a glazed dome: hot water pipes were run around the base of the latter in an ineffectual effort to ensure the space didn't grow too cold. In recent years, Kilcooley has stood empty with damp and decay becoming ever more prevalent.

Kilcooley's vast interiors date from the early 1840s when the house had to be extensively renovated, following a fire started by a vengeful butler. The galleried, two-storey entrance hall leads to a series of reception rooms with views across the garden to the ruins of a Medieval Cistercian abbey.

The famous poem Caoine Cill Chaise (A Lament for Kilcash) expresses dismay at the destruction of the area's ancient woodlands, yet this was carried out on the instructions of the castle's owner, Walter Butler, who was in need of cash to pay for work to another of his properties, Kilkenny Castle.

Kilcash COUNTY TIPPERARY

The spoliation of Kilcash, County Tipperary provided the inspiration for one of the most famous poems in the Irish language: *Caoine Cill Chaise* (A Lament for Kilcash) mourns the passing of Margaret Butler in 1744. A daughter of the seventh Earl of Clanricarde, Margaret married first Bryan Magennis, fifth Viscount Iveagh and after his death Colonel Thomas Butler, who lived at Kilcash. The castle is probably a sixteenth-century tower house built either by the Butlers or by the de Vale (Wall) family who lived here before them. The poem uses Margaret Butler's death to mourn the loss of the woods that once surrounded Kilcash, and with them the destruction of the old Gaelic way of life. For a long time, the work was attributed to a Roman Catholic priest, John Lane, who was based at nearby Carrick-on-Suir and whose education had been paid for by Margaret Butler. However, he died in 1776 and the timber from Kilcash was not advertized for sale until over 20 years later. It transpires that the Butlers were responsible for the disappearance of the old woodland. Toward the end of the eighteenth century, having once more acquired the title Earl of Ormonde, they moved to Kilkenny Castle and lavishly refurbished the building and its demesne. It was Walter Butler, future first Marquess of Ormonde, who—in need of cash—decided to cut down the woods of Kilcash. The Lament is likely to have been written toward the middle of the nineteenth century, by which time the castle itself had been abandoned and begun falling into disrepair.

Despite its size and location close to Cork city, relatively little is known about Kilcrea. In 1851 the house and some 422 acres were advertised for sale and appear to have been bought by the Hawkes family: by the 1870s the estate of John Devonsher Hawkes of Kilcrea was given as amounting to 2,029 acres, but thereafter its history grows more obscure.

Kilcrea COUNTY CORK

There are three ruins in close proximity to each other at Kilcrea. The best-known is a former Franciscan friary dating from the 1460s: it was built on or near an older religious settlement believed to have been founded by Saint Cere or Cyra. The placename Kilcrea derives from this: Cill Chre (Cell of Cyra). The Franciscans were brought here by Cormac Láidir Mór, Lord of Muskerry, then head of the McCarthy clan. Within sight of the friary and around the same time, he erected a five-storey tower house, the ruins of which, as Coyne and Wills wrote in *The Scenery and Antiquities of Ireland* (1841), "evince it to have been a place of considerable extent and rude magnificence." The histories of these two buildings are reasonably well known, but not so that of a more recent

house close by. From what remains, it looks to have been built in the eighteenth century and, like many other such residences in this area of Ireland, the external walls were at least part-covered in slate for extra insulation. In 1786 William Wilson's *The Post-Chaise Companion* noted the ruins of the friary and castle, near to which was a house called Snugborough, the residence of a Mr. Keeffe. By the time of Griffith's Valuation in the 1850s, Robert Gibbons was given as the occupier of Kilcrea House. Other names are listed as subsequent residents and the condition of the building indicates it was used until relatively recently. Now, unroofed and with trees growing inside the house, it has joined its neighbors to form a trio of ruins.

Heathfield COUNTY CORK

Heathfield dates from c.1780 and, as far as the interior is concerned, follows the period's standard design and layout. Its exterior, on the other hand, is distinctly non-conformist. The entrance front, although facing east, is a blank rubble wall except for one small door placed off-center. Meanwhile, the weather-slated rear elevation likewise has just a single point of entry—at basement level—and only two windows (one now blocked) placed on the upper floor. What can be the explanation for such an odd arrangement, which must have made the rooms inside rather dark? Did the original builder fear civil disturbance, and therefore minimize points of access to the building? Heathfield's defensive character certainly served it well in the mid-1830s when County Cork experienced considerable upheaval during the Tithe Wars, a campaign against paying money to the Church of Ireland. In March 1834 the house's then-occupant Henry Bastable was woken by a large group of men surrounding Heathfield, calling on him to hand over any weapons he might have. Through one of the few windows, Bastable duly proffered his only gun. Next the men wanted money, initially demanding £5. After some negotiation, 50 shillings was agreed upon and given to them. The group then departed, but returned a short time later to give back the gun: Bastable believed this was because it was a new kind of device, the operating mechanism unfamiliar—and therefore of no use—to his nocturnal visitors. Heathfield was occupied until the 1970s but has since fallen into a poor condition. The dining-room floor has completely collapsed and other parts of the building are vulnerable, but enough survives to show it was evidently built for a gentleman farmer who wished to emulate the lifestyle enjoyed by wealthier members of society.

The east-facing entrance front of Heathfield is a blank rubble wall except for one small door placed off-center. A wing, now ruinous, stands on the north-east corner: perhaps there was once another on the other side of the building, thereby creating a miniature Palladian house.

Lackeen COUNTY TIPPERARY

Lackeen Castle is a four-storey tower house built by the Ua Cinneides, a name later anglicized to Kennedy. Although they were forced to surrender the building to English forces in 1653, the family later regained possession of the property. In 1735, while undertaking work on the tower house, John O'Kennedy discovered an ancient manuscript hidden inside one of its walls. Today known as the *Stowe Missal*, the work was written in Latin in the late eighth or early ninth century, but in the mid-eleventh century had been annotated and some additional pages written in Irish. By that date the manuscript seems to have come into the safekeeping of a monastery at nearby Lorrha, remaining there until the dissolution of such establishments in the mid-sixteenth century; most likely the manuscript was then concealed for safekeeping at Lackeen Castle. Following its rediscovery, the missal entered the collection of Irish antiquarian Charles O'Conor. In 1798, his grandson, a Roman Catholic priest also called Charles O'Conor, was invited to become chaplain to the first Marchioness of Buckingham and to organize and translate a collection of historic material kept at her husband's house, Stowe in Buckinghamshire. On moving to England, the younger O'Conor brought with him 59 of his grandfather's manuscripts, including the missal found at Lackeen. This remained at Stowe until the entire collection was sold to the fourth Earl of Ashburnham in 1849: in turn his son sold all the manuscripts to the British Government, which returned relevant material to Ireland. The *Stowe Missal* is now in the possession of the Royal Irish Academy. Adjacent to Lackeen Castle and on the edge of the bawn wall is a group of domestic buildings, which look to be from the seventeenth and early eighteenth centuries: it would seem at least some of these were erected in the aftermath of 1660 when peace, for a time, returned to Ireland. All are now in a ruinous state.

Lackeen was built for the Ua Cinneides, their name being the Irish word for "Helmeted Head" (it being said that members of the family were the first people in Ireland to wear helmets when going into battle against the Vikings). The name was later anglicized to Kennedy and the family remains widespread in this part of north Tipperary.

New Hall COUNTY CLARE

County Clare folklore tells how a member of the O'Brien family, living in a large house close to Killone Lake, noticed supplies of wine in his cellar being inexplicably depleted. Determined to catch the culprit, one night he stayed up late and discovered the perpetrator was a mermaid who swam upstream to the house from the lake. Recovering from his surprise, he shot the creature and wounded her. Bleeding profusely and screaming in pain, the mermaid fled, but not before delivering a curse: "As the mermaid goes on the sea/ So shall the race of O'Briens pass away/ Till they leave Killone in wild weeds." It was also said that every seven years the lake turned red, an evocation of the mermaid's blood. The cellars at Newhall are supposed to contain a heavily enclosed recess, which was where the thieving mermaid tried to enter. The O'Briens had a long association with this site, having founded an Augustinian nunnery on the banks of Killone Lake around 1190, and even after its dissolution, the family still owned the land here. It is likely the rear section of New Hall was built by one of them, either in the late seventeenth or early eighteenth century. In the 1760s, the house and surrounding estate were bought by Charles MacDonnell from his cousin Edward O'Brien. MacDonnell added a new block to the front of the existing building, this work perhaps designed by local amateur architect Francis Bindon. The MacDonnells remained in residence until the 1920s, after which New Hall was acquired by a farming family from neighboring County Galway. After standing vacant for some years, the house was sold in June 2016 and, one hopes, will now undergo a necessary program of restoration.

Right and overleaf *In the 1760s New Hall was given a brick-fronted façade, built onto what was probably a seventeenth-century long house of rubble stone. Indoors, this means long corridors meander along several floors and give access to successive rooms, many of them in poor condition.*

Lakeview COUNTY CORK

Lakeview looks to be of early nineteenth-century origin, the core of the house being a simple villa of two storeys and three bays. Single-storey wings were added later, one serving as the main entrance, the other as a bow-window in what was probably the drawing room. The property was for a long time owned by the Hallinans, a prosperous Roman Catholic family which had made its money in milling. Its most prominent member was Sir Eric Hallinan, educated at Downside School and Trinity College, Dublin before becoming a barrister. Entering the British Colonial Service, he first worked in Nigeria before acting as Attorney-General in the Bahamas during the Second World War. Subsequently Attorney-General of Nigeria, he was then appointed Chief Justice of Cyprus, in which capacity he achieved notoriety for presiding over the trial of Michalis Karaolis, a member of the Greek Cyrpiot

nationalist guerrilla organization EOKA: found guilty of the murder of a police officer, despite global appeals for mercy Karaolis was hanged in 1956. Lakeview remained in use as a private residence until the beginning of the present century. In 2005 the property and surrounding land were sold for £26 million, after which plans were prepared for building some 430 apartments and houses on the site. Economic recession put an end to the scheme, and for the past decade the house has stood empty and growing ever-more dilapidated.

Situated less than 15 miles from the center of Cork city, Lakeview was sold at the height of the economic boom in expectation that the land on which the house stands would be extensively developed. Then recession came, and ever since the building has grown steadily more dilapidated, a monument to the Celtic Tiger era.

CHAPTER 3

CONNACHT

"To Hell or to Connacht" is a well-known expression in Ireland, popularly attributed to the English Commonwealth's 1652 Act of Settlement. This act saw native Irish people who had fought against the government dispossessed of their land and required to move to the west of the country. This is the province known as Connacht, often scenically beautiful but of low agricultural merit, hence the analogy with Hell. Its name derives from the Irish word *Connachta*, often thought to refer to a group of ancient Irish dynasties ruling this part of the country and claiming descent from a legendary High King of Ireland, Conn of the Hundred Battles. As so often, the territory controlled by the Connachta was fluid, but today the province covers Counties Galway, Leitrim, Mayo, Roscommon, and Sligo. Connacht has the highest percentage of Irish-speakers in the country, between 5-10 percent of its residents, but at just over 540,000 people is Ireland's least populated province (prior to the Great Famine, the Census of 1841 gave a figure of more than 1.4 million for the same part of the country).

Clonfert Palace

COUNTY GALWAY

Today a tiny village in the middle of flat countryside, it is hard to believe that Clonfert once had a resident population of some 3,000 monks, or that in the mid-twentieth century it was home to one of Britain's most infamous politicians. An exquisite pocket cathedral, its west façade dominated by an elaborately carved Hiberno-Romanesque doorcase, testifies to the area's former renown as the burial place of the early Irish Saint Brendan. Known as Brendan the Voyager, he is said to have made an epic sea journey with a number of companions, one that took seven years and brought them across the Atlantic to the shores of North America. References to an account of this voyage occur as early as the ninth century, although extant texts of the *Navigatio sancti Brendani abbatis* (Voyage of Saint Brendan the Abbot) are somewhat later. A shorter voyage was made by the former leader of the British Union of Fascists, Sir Oswald Mosley, in 1951. Keen to escape from ongoing hostility in England, together with his wife Diana (née Mitford) and their two sons, he moved from England into the old Bishop's Palace in Clonfert. Dating from the seventeenth century, the house was extensively renovated by the Mosleys but they were able to enjoy the place for less than three years before it was gutted by fire in December 1954. The building has remained a ruin ever since.

Following the merger of Clonfert with a number of other Church of Ireland dioceses in 1834, the former Bishop's Palace became a private residence, its last owner being Sir Oswald Mosley and his wife Diana. They had barely completed refurbishment of the house when it was almost totally destroyed by fire in 1954.

Much of what now constitutes Bunowen Castle dates from the first half of the 1830s when Augustus John O'Neill enlarged and embellished the old building. He did not enjoy the property for long, having to sell it less than 20 years later in the aftermath of the Great Famine.

Bunowen Castle COUNTY GALWAY

The O'Flaherty family are descended from one Flaithbheartach mac Eimhin who originally settled on the eastern side of what is now County Galway. Later they were driven further west and came to control much of Connemara. But like many other such tribes, they were almost constantly striving to expand the area under their authority and it is said the Medieval walls of Galway city carried the inscription "From the ferocious O'Flahertys O Lord Deliver Us." By this time, one of their strongholds was Bunowen Castle, County Galway strategically located by the Hill of Doon and overlooking the Atlantic Ocean. In the sixteenth century this part of the country was controlled by Dónal "an Chogaidh" Ó Flaithbheartaigh (Donal of the Battle) who in 1546 married Gráinne, daughter of Eoghan Dubhdara Ó Máille, chief of the Ó Máille clan in neighboring County

Mayo: she is also known as Grace O'Malley, the Pirate Queen. The castle remained in the family's ownership until the 1650s when it was captured by the Cromwellian army and given to Arthur Geoghegan, whose own lands in County Westmeath had been taken from him. In 1808 John David Geoghegan of Bunowen petitioned the government for permission to change his surname: he believed himself descended from the prehistoric Irish king Niall of the Nine Hostages and therefore wished to take the name of O'Neill. His son, Augustus John O'Neill, embarked on an ambitious building program to enlarge the house but was forced to sell up after the Great Famine. Thereafter used as a summer residence, the castle was intact a century ago but at some later date abandoned. It now stands a gaunt ruin gazing out to the Atlantic.

Garbally Court COUNTY GALWAY

In July 1889 William Frederick Le Poer Trench, Viscount Dunlo, heir to the Earldom of Clancarty, wed music-hall entertainer Belle Bilton, much to the fury of his father. The latter banished his son to Australia and insisted he petition for a divorce, but the couple remained married and two years later the earl died, and so Belle duly became Countess of Clancarty. After bearing five children, she died of cancer in 1906: a year later her husband was declared bankrupt. It was a far cry from the position the family had occupied only a century earlier. The Trenches were of French Huguenot origin, their forebear moving to Ireland in the early 1630s and buying large amounts of land in the area of east County Galway. Advantageous marriages in the eighteenth century increased the size of the estate and eventually led to the acquisition of a peerage. In 1815 the second Earl of Clancarty played a major role at the Congress of Vienna; for his role as Ambassador to the Netherlands, he was awarded the Dutch hereditary title of Marquess of Heusden by King Willem I. It was the second earl who commissioned a new house at Garbally from Thomas Cundy, the English architect's only major work in Ireland. In 1923 the property was sold to the local Roman Catholic diocese and has served as a secondary school ever since. While the main house remains occupied, the handsome yards some distance away have been allowed to fall into their present miserable condition.

Garbally today belongs to the Roman Catholic church which is ironic since the second Earl of Clancarty, who built the present house, was a staunch Protestant (one of his younger brothers served as the Church of Ireland Archbishop of Tuam) and voted against the Catholic Emancipation Act of 1829.

When the Rev. Daniel Beaufort visited Tyrone House in 1788 he described it as being "large and new but very bleak and too high though some low woods about it." Little has changed since then, and what remains of the building continues to look raw and exposed in the midst of flat countryside.

Tyrone House COUNTY GALWAY

In March 1912 Violet Martin, one half of the literary duo Somerville and Ross, wrote to her writing partner Edith Somerville about a visit to Tyrone House, describing it as a larger and grander version of her own home. "It is on a long promontory by the sea and there rioted three or four generations of St. Georges—living with country-women, occasionally marrying them, all illegitimate four times over. No so long ago eight of these awful half-peasant families roosted together in that lovely house, and fought, and barricaded and drank, till the police had to intervene—about 150 years ago a very grand Lady Harriet St. Lawrence married a St. George, and lived there, and was so corroded with pride that she would not allow her daughters to associate with the Galway people. She lived to see them marry two men in the yard. Yesterday as we left an old Miss St. George, daughter of the last owner, was at the door in a donkey trap—she lives near, in a bit of the castle, and since her people died she will not go into Tyrone House, or into the enormous yard, or the beautiful old garden. She was a strange mixture of distinction and commonness, like her breeding, and it was very sad to see her at the door of that great house— If we dare to write up that subject!" Gutted by fire in 1920 during the War of Independence, Tyrone House provided the inspiration for Somerville and Ross's novel *The Big House of Inver,* published in 1925.

Glenlossera Lodge

COUNTY MAYO

In 1849 the Westminster Parliament established an organization called the Encumbered Estates' Court. This body's purpose was to facilitate the sale of insolvent Irish estates, the owners of which had become hopelessly indebted during the years of the Great Famine (1845–48). The Court could sell lands at the request of either the owner or, as was frequently the case, somebody who had a claim on it via an unpaid mortgage. Following the sale, the proceeds were distributed among creditors, the new owners being granted clear title. Within a decade over five million acres worth some £21 million had so changed hands. Among those making a purchase was the wonderfully named Zachary Mudge, who in January 1854 paid the Encumbered Estates' Court £2,490 for an estate of 3,635 acres in County Mayo. Mudge, whose father had been an admiral in the British Navy, subsequently built a lodge at Glenlossera using local sandstone with yellow brick for the door- and windowcases. Since his main properties were in Devon and Cornwall, Mudge seems never to have spent much time here. In 1882, for example, the house was rented to Lady Florence Dixie, daughter of the Eighth Marquess of Queensberry (and aunt of Oscar Wilde's lover, Lord Alfred Douglas). Gradually the estate was sold, much of it to the Land Commission, and finally the house itself passed into other hands in the late 1920s. In recent years Glenlossera Lodge was offered for sale, but without a new owner the place has fallen into serious disrepair.

Unoccupied for several decades, in 2008 permission was granted for the restoration of Glenlossera Lodge. However that work does not seem to have proceeded very far and in the intervening years the building has suffered further decay.

Killegar COUNTY LEITRIM

In 1955, John Godley, third Lord Kilbracken, wrote, "It's easy to love Killegar, as I realised more than ever when I came here for the first time after my father's death. I can imagine selling it when I'm in Portofino, or Manhattan, or Paris (and imagine the villa, penthouse or atelier I'll buy instead)…" He never did so, his love for the place overwhelming any urge to make money. Kilbracken, journalist and bon viveur, was throughout the course of a long life the embodiment of the impoverished Irish peer possessed of big house and small income. A man of intelligence and charm, his various books are to be recommended for their ability to make sundry travails sound highly entertaining. For example, in *Living like a Lord* (1955) he devotes a chapter to recounting how he almost came to play the part of Ishmael in John Huston's *Moby Dick*. Typically, as a result of amusing the director one night over dinner, he found himself caught up in a six-month maelstrom of screen tests and costume

fittings before eventually being relegated to the part of an extra carrying a live pig onto a vessel. However, owing to technical issues the scene had to be re-shot with someone else as pig carrier. Thus he never made the final cut, although he did work as a supplementary script writer, for which—naturally in his narrative—he received no screen credit. With regard to Killegar, the greatest challenge Kilbracken faced occurred in 1970 when the house was gutted by fire. A rebuilding program followed, testament to his devotion, but sadly many of the contents were forever lost. He struggled on and then, since his death in 2006, Killegar has been occupied by his second wife Sue and their son Seán. It remains as much a battle as ever to keep the house from falling into desolation. With little land (and proportionately little income), Killegar is at a turning point in its fortunes: the last big house in County Leitrim to remain in the hands of the original family… but for how much longer?

Dating from the second decade of the nineteenth century, Killegar has been home to the Godleys for the past two centuries. Despite valiant efforts by present members of the family, sections of the house are already ruinous and assistance is needed to stem further decay.

Dunsandle COUNTY GALWAY

In 1786 William Wilson in *The Post-Chaise Companion or Traveller's Directory Through Ireland* described Dunsandle, County Galway, as a "most magnificent and beautiful seat, with ample demesnes of the Rt. Hon. Denis Daly." A handful of late nineteenth-/early twentieth-century photographs give an idea of how the interiors once looked. The saloon had elaborate and very pretty rococo plasterwork on the walls, while the drawing room had an Adamesque ceiling. The entrance hall contained later plasterwork almost certainly designed by James Wyatt. (In 1780 Denis Daly had married the heiress of the first Lord Farnham, who commissioned Wyatt to work on his house.) Staircases with carved balusters rose on either side of the hall, leading to bedrooms and sitting rooms on the first floor. A surviving inventory from 1911 shows that the house's contents were just as splendid. The family remained in situ until the middle of the last century. In 1950 Major Bowes Daly divorced his first wife to marry Melosine Hanbury (née Cary-Barnard), with whom he had hitherto been joint Master of the Galway Blazers. Mrs Hanbury had already had two husbands, her first Wing Commander Marcus Trundle being in the news some years ago when it was revealed that in the mid-1930s London police reported he was the secret lover of Wallis Simpson. Whatever the truth about that story, it appears Major Daly's divorce and re-marriage caused a stir in County Galway in the early 1950s with local Catholic clergy advising farmers to boycott the hunt. Eventually the Dalys sold the contents of Dunsandle and moved to Africa. The house was unroofed in 1958.

Moore Hall COUNTY MAYO

Moore Hall is widely believed to have been designed by Waterford architect John Roberts, thought also responsible for Tyrone House, County Galway (see page 125), likewise now a ruin. In the middle of the eighteenth century George Moore moved to Spain where he prospered in the wine export business. In addition he manufactured iodine, a valuable commodity at the time, and shipped seaweed from Galway for its production, owning a fleet of vessels for this purpose. Having made a fortune, George Moore returned to Ireland and bought land to create an estate of some 12,500 acres. He commissioned a residence to be built on Muckloon Hill with wonderful views across Lough Carra below. Fronted in cut limestone, Moore Hall stands three storeys over sunken basement, the façade centered on a single-bay breakfront with Doric portico below the first-floor Venetian window. A date stone indicates it was completed in 1795, three years before Ireland erupted in rebellion. Among those who took part was George Moore's eldest son John, who after being schooled at Douai had studied law in Paris and London. On August 31st 1798 the French General Jean Joseph Amable Humbert issued a decree proclaiming John Moore "President of the Government of the Province of Connacht." However, within weeks the British authorities had crushed the rebellion and captured Moore, who died the following year while en route to the east coast where he was due to be deported. George Moore, having spent some £2,500 attempting to secure his heir's release, had died just a month earlier. Despite this pedigree, Moore Hall was burnt in February 1923 during the Irish Civil War. In January 2018 the local county council announced it had purchased the house and surrounding 80 acres to develop as a nature reserve and tourist attraction.

Concealed by encroaching trees in this photograph, an abacus or tablet in the center of the house's parapet carried the Moore family motto: Fortis cadere cedere non potest. *Translating as "The brave may fall but never yield" it is apposite for Moore Hall which, despite being burnt out in 1923, has never yet yielded to the elements.*

Pallas Castle and its lands passed into the ownership of the Nugent family in the mid-seventeenth century and they lived in these buildings until the late 1790s when a new house was commissioned from the amateur architect William Leeson. Following the sale of its contents, the latter was entirely demolished in 1945, so only the older structures still stand.

Pallas Castle COUNTY GALWAY

Pallas Castle is believed to date from c.1500 when it was built by a branch of the Burke family, descendants of the Norman de Burghs, the first of whom, William de Burgh, had seized territory in this part of the country and in 1203 called himself Lord of Connacht. Rising five storeys, the tower stands within a bawn wall, access to which is through an east-facing two-storey gatehouse flanked by similarly proportioned turrets. Immediately adjacent to the tower house on the west side are portions of a seventeenth-century house, its gable end built into the bawn wall, through which a separate entrance was created. The Burkes remained in possession of Pallas until the mid-seventeenth century when, like many other families who had risen against the Commonwealth army, they were dispossessed of their lands and moved further west. The same fate befell another ancient family of

Norman origins, the Nugents, formerly Barons Delvin but since 1621 Earls of Westmeath. They too were required to depart their original property and move west, being given part of the former Burke estate including Pallas. Following the restoration of Charles II in 1660, the second Earl of Westmeath was allowed to return to his ancestral lands and those in County Galway bestowed on his second son, the Hon. Thomas Nugent, created Baron Nugent of Riverston by James II in 1689. As a Roman Catholic and Jacobite he went into exile, dying in 1715, but his sons conformed to the established church and so were able to retain both the family title and estates. Their descendants remained at Pallas until the 1930s, living in a very large house dating from the late eighteenth century: this was demolished in 1945 and no trace of it remains on the site.

Ardfry COUNTY GALWAY

Irish landlords, that small band of men who once owned the greater part of the country, do not enjoy a good reputation. Judged to have been rapacious and, often worse in the popular mind, foreign, it cannot be denied that many of their number put personal interest ahead of concern for the condition of tenants. However, it would be wrong to tar all landlords with the same brush, since a few of them sought to improve the circumstances of those under their care. Among this band none was more unusual than Joseph Henry Blake, third Lord Wallscourt of Ardfry, County Galway. While publicly applauded for the concern he displayed for his tenants, in his own home Lord Wallscourt showed a different character. In 1846, after more than 20 years of marriage, his heiress wife sought a divorce "by reason of his cruelty and adultery," citing several instances when her husband had assaulted her. He was known to be a man of considerable strength and, when young, had been a keen boxer. More peculiarly he liked to walk about his house wearing no clothes:

eventually Lady Wallscourt persuaded him carry a cowbell in his hand when nude so maidservants had notice of his imminent arrival. Within three years of the divorce Lord Wallscourt had died and Ardfry was inherited by his only surviving son, a man so small and diffident that he was known in the vicinity as "the lordeen": Nationalist politician T.P. O'Connor remembered meeting "a tiny little man, sad, deprecatory, almost timid in manner." This may have been because he was oppressed by money worries, especially following his second marriage. His new wife turned out to be a gambler. Matters grew worse during the lifetime of the fifth and last Lord Wallscourt, a hopeless drunk who was declared bankrupt just weeks before his death in 1920. Members of the family struggled on for another few decades but by 1973 director John Huston was able to use Ardfry in his film *The Mackintosh Man*, for which the house was reroofed and windowed, then spectacularly set on fire. The remains were most recently offered for sale in 2015.

Kiltullagh

COUNTY GALWAY

Believed to date from the late seventeenth or early eighteenth centuries, Kiltullagh belonged to a branch of the d'Arcy family, one of the mercantile Tribes of Galway that ran the city during the Middle Ages. From the early sixteenth century onward they gradually acquired parcels of land in the countryside and metamorphosed into gentry, although this process was not without setbacks. The lawyer Patrick d'Arcy was a key figure on the Roman Catholic side during the Confederate Wars of 1641–52, in the former year writing his *Argument*, which insisted that "no parliament but an Irish one can properly legislate for Ireland" and later helping to draw up a Constitution for the Confederacy. In the aftermath of that side's defeat, he lost his lands but most of these were restored to his heir, James d'Arcy. The family owned over 18,750 acres, divided between Kiltullagh and a second estate further west, before everything was lost in the aftermath of the Great Famine when the property was sold by the Encumbered Estates' Court. (The last of the family to own the property, Hyacinth d'Arcy, subsequently became a Church of Ireland clergyman). Kiltullagh was seemingly occupied by the family until the second decade of the nineteenth century when John d'Arcy, following the death of his first wife, moved to Clifden where he founded the present town of the same name and built a new residence, Clifden Castle (now also a ruin). Thereafter Kiltullagh was rented to tenants and at some date before 1850 gutted by fire. The house was never rebuilt and stood a ruin, but some years ago work was undertaken on the site to secure what remained. However, this enterprise appears to have halted and the interior remains filled with scaffolding.

Roscommon Castle COUNTY ROSCOMMON

Work began on the construction of Roscommon Castle in 1269 on the instructions of the Anglo-Norman knight Roger de Ufford, Justiciar (or chief governor) of Ireland for Henry III. There were constant setbacks due to attacks by Aedh O'Conor, King of Connacht and by the mid-fourteenth century the castle had passed into the hands of his descendants who remained in occupancy for the next 200 years. In 1569 the then O'Conor Don Diarmaid mac Cairbre surrendered Roscommon Castle to Sir Henry Sidney, Lord Deputy of Ireland. Eight years later the building and 17,000 acres were granted by the English Government to Sir Nicholas Malby, Governor (later Lord President) of Connacht. Malby fundamentally altered the appearance of the castle by transforming it into a Renaissance fortified mansion. The northern side, which had never been of stone, was made into a three-storey domestic dwelling linked to the eastern range to form

an L-shaped block: large stone mullion windows were inserted into the upper floors of the latter to admit more light than had hitherto been the case. Following Malby's death in 1584, the castle was inherited by a son reported to have been slain during a battle against the Irish at Aughrim in January 1603. But even before that date Roscommon Castle had once more been subject to attack, besieged by Hugh O'Donnell for three months in 1596 and again assaulted in 1599. It changed hands on a couple of occasions during the Confederate Wars of the 1640s before being taken by a Cromwellian force in 1652. In the aftermath of this event, some of the defensive features may have been removed, but further damage was apparently done to the structure during the Williamite Wars of the early 1690s. Since then it has stood in a state of decay.

In his Statistical Survey of the County of Roscommon (1832), Isaac Weld wrote that the ruins of Roscommon Castle "make a grand and noble appearance…In the evening, when the gleams of the setting sun are seen darting through the ruined casements and narrow loop holes, whilst the main body of the ruins remains involved in deep shade, the effect of the scene is more than usually impressive."

Elphin Palace COUNTY ROSCOMMON

Writing to his daughter Alicia in May 1747, Edward Synge, Bishop of Elphin, County Roscommon, described the new residence he was then building: "The Scaffolding is all down, and the House almost pointed, and It's figure is vastly more beautifull [sic] than I expected it would be. Conceited people may censure its plainess. But I don't wish it any further ornament than it has. As far as I can yet judge, the inside will be very commodious and comfortable." He had to wait a further two years to find out whether or not this was the case, but in early June 1749 Synge was finally able to advise Alicia, "The House is as dry as you could wish. I lay last night as well and as Warm as ever I did in my life, and quite free from the only nuisance I fear'd, the smell of paint and am, I bless God, as well to day, as I was, when I wrote from Palmer's…" The design of the Bishop's Palace at Elphin is attributed to Dublin architect Michael Wills, not least because a "Mr Wills' is frequently mentioned in Synge's correspondence in relation to the house's construction. Very much in

the Irish Palladian mode, it consisted of a three-storey, east-facing central block, its first-floor Venetian window of the same style and proportions as the main entrance below: quadrants linked this building to wings on either side. Unfortunately the main block was destroyed by an accidental fire in 1911 and subsequently demolished, leaving the quadrants and wings on either side looking rather lost. In recent years, the south wing has been restored as a family residence. However, its match to the north is a ruin with a bungalow built immediately in front, making the site look even more lopsided.

Although its wings survive in different states of repair, the central block of Bishop Edward Synge's palace built in the 1740s was demolished after a fire in 1911. The nearby cathedral, also constructed in the eighteenth century, was likewise knocked down in the 1960s.

CHAPTER 4

ULSTER

Covering the northern part of the island, Ulster is Ireland's largest
province after Munster. The province has had a troubled history: for
almost a century, Ulster has been divided, with six of its counties
comprising Northern Ireland and the other three being part of the Irish
Republic. Throughout the Middle Ages, it remained least affected by
Norman or English settlers and was dominated by successive members
of the indigenous O'Neill and O'Donnell families. However, following their
defeat and departure into exile at the start of the seventeenth century,
official government policy encouraged extensive colonization of the
province by English-speaking Protestants, many of them from Scotland:
in consequence, much of the old Gaelic culture was obliterated. In the
eighteenth century, Ulster enjoyed prosperity thanks to the rise of the
linen industry. This continued into the nineteenth century when Belfast
became an important port and a center of ship-building (it was here
that the Titanic was constructed). The more recent decline of both the
linen and ship-building industries helps to explain why so many of these
properties are now in a ruinous condition.

Termon Castle

COUNTY DONEGAL

Myler McGrath is unique in Irish history for having managed to serve simultaneously as a prelate of both the Roman Catholic and Anglican churches. Born c.1523, McGrath was a member of an old Ulster family, many of whom attained high clerical office. First becoming a Franciscan friar, he moved to Rome where in 1565 Pope Pius IV appointed him Bishop of Down and Connor in Ireland. However, on returning to his native country, he conformed to the Established (Protestant) church and was duly appointed first Bishop of Clogher in 1570 and then a year later Archbishop of Cashel. Meanwhile, he remained as Catholic Bishop of Down and Connor until removed from the position on the grounds of heresy in 1580. By this time he had married and fathered at least eight children. It is said he once asked his wife—who remained Catholic—why she would not eat meat on Fridays, to which she replied that to do so would be a sin. "Surely," he replied, "you committed a far greater sin in coming to the bed of me a friar." McGrath, who only died in 1623 when aged 100, was responsible for building this castle on his family's lands. Believed to date from the early seventeenth century, it was attacked by General Ireton during the Confederate Wars of the 1640s and so badly damaged that the building was never occupied again.

Forever interested in bettering himself and his substantial family, the builder of Termon Castle, Myler McGrath, not only acquired the Diocese of Cashel but, after complaining its annual income was insufficient, also became Bishop of Waterford and Lismore.

Castle Irvine COUNTY FERMANAGH

Originally built in the second decade of the seventeenth century, Castle Irvine, sometimes known as Necarne Castle, assumed its present appearance in the 1830s when architect John Benjamin Keane revamped the building in the Tudor-Gothic idiom. A new range was added in front of the old castle, of five bays with an arcaded central porch and octagonal turrets at the corners. Further towers and crenellations were scattered liberally elsewhere, so that the whole building became an elaborate Gothic fantasy. However, while the exterior of Castle Irvine was in one style, the interiors adopted another, being strictly Classical. The entrance hall, for example, was flanked by red scagliola columns with Corinthian columns. During the Second World War the castle was used as a military hospital by British and American forces but thereafter left unoccupied. Following the death of its last private owner, in 1976 the building and surrounding estate were put up for sale and bought first by a local entrepreneur before being acquired in 1987 for about £300,000 by the local district council which then spent a further £4 million developing equestrian facilities on the site, including a 300-seat indoor arena, 80 stables, 16 bedrooms, two dressage arenas, and courses for cross-country, point-to-point, and steeplechase. Throughout this time no funds were spent on the old castle which, despite being a listed building in the care of the council, deteriorated to the point where it is now just a shell: as one of the authority's officials told the BBC in 2016 "Unfortunately a use for the castle has not been found and it would take a very serious amount of money to put it back together." It is hard to imagine who might now want to spend such money for what has become a large and derelict white elephant.

Although still used as a family home until the outbreak of the Second World War, Castle Irvine's decline began in 1922 when Major Charles Cockburn D'Arcy-Irvine gave up living in the place: his only son, Captain Charles William D'Arcy-Irvine, had been killed in the Dardanelles seven years earlier.

Wardtown Castle COUNTY DONEGAL

The early seventeenth-century Plantation of Ulster saw that part of the country carved up between a number of different parties, including soldiers and other adventurers, the Established Church, and Trinity College, Dublin. The last of these owned some 700 acres where Wardtown Castle stands and leased it in 1616 to the Folliott family, who already held other land in the vicinity. When the lease was renewed in 1733 it came with the stipulation that the Folliotts had to build "within ten years, a house of lime and stone forty foot by eighteen foot and one and a half storeys high." In fact the residence constructed by General John Folliott is very much larger than demanded. Wardtown Castle is of three storeys over raised basement, with three half-round towers on the front and one in the center of the rear. On the ground floor, the central entrance hall has apsed ends and is flanked by two large rooms, each measuring 21 feet square with windows on either side. Off these, to the front are perfectly round rooms both 13 feet in diameter: on their domed ceilings traces of delicate plasterwork survive (likewise some of the more robust plaster paneling in the former drawing room also remains). Behind the round rooms and similarly accessed from the reception areas are identically proportioned square stair halls, on the walls of which can still be seen evidence of their former purpose. Rigorously governed by symmetry, the building may have been designed or inspired by Sir Edward Lovett Pearce, although he died in1733 and building work is only supposed to have begun at the end of that decade. General Folliott having no children, Wardtown passed to cousins and by the start of the last century it had ceased to be occupied, gradually slipping into ruin.

These pages and overleaf *The center of Wardtown Castle appears to have been occupied by a great entrance hall, to right and left of which ran a series of reception rooms concluding at the front in domed rotundas and to the rear in a pair of staircases. Traces of surviving plasterwork give some sense of how the interiors once looked.*

Dartrey COUNTY MONAGHAN

The Yorkshire Dawson family moved to Ireland during the reign of Elizabeth I, Thomas Dawson becoming a Burgess of Armagh. Subsequently in the mid-seventeenth century his descendant Richard Dawson assembled the nucleus of what would become a substantial estate in County Monaghan. Through judicious marriages, the Dawsons became steadily richer and in the 1770s Thomas Dawson built a fine house in what was now called Dawson's Grove. He also acquired a London residence, Cremorne House in Chelsea, where the garden designer Nathaniel Richmond was commissioned to lay out the grounds (although the house is long gone, this is now the site of Cremorne Gardens, just down river from Battersea Bridge). Around the same time Thomas Dawson was created Baron Dartrey of Dawson's Grove, and in June 1785 Viscount Cremorne. On the death of his first wife, Lady Anne Fermor, Dawson built a splendid domed mausoleum in her memory, designed by James Wyatt and containing a large white marble sculptural group

carved by Joseph Wilton. In the late 1840s Richard Dawson, the third Lord Cremorne (and first Earl of Dartrey), embarked on a new building program, replacing the Georgian house with an immense Elizabethan Revival mansion. Alas, barely a century later it was all torn down and nothing remains except this curved eighteenth-century range of stables overlooking Lough Dromore. The Dartrey Mausoleum has been meticulously restored in recent years, and the stables look set to require their own memorial soon.

The long redbrick stable range at Dartrey dates from around 1760 or possibly earlier and is picturesquely sited close to Lough Dromore. Originally the Doric columns in the interiors supported brick vaults but the latter were destroyed in 2012, leaving what remains even more vulnerable to the elements.

Mount Panther is a relatively recent ruin, having survived intact until half a century ago. In June 1963 Princess Margaret and her husband, the Earl of Snowdon, visited the house to see the Adamesque plasterwork then covering the walls and ceiling of the ballroom. Today only fragments of this survive.

Mount Panther COUNTY DOWN

One of the most talented and energetic women of the eighteenth century, Mary Delany (née Granville) spent a quarter century in Ireland following her marriage in 1743 to the cleric Patrick Delany. A year later her husband was appointed Dean of Down and accordingly the couple, who otherwise lived on the outskirts of Dublin, annually traveled north to spend time in the diocese. For many years they rented a house called Mount Panther, a few miles outside Down. Mrs Delany expended as much time and care on the building's preparation for these visits as she did on everything else, writing on arrival at the house to her beloved sister, Anne Dewes, in July 1750, "You who have had the experience of such affairs, can figure to yourself my present bustle—trunks, hampers, unpacking, hay flying all over the house; everybody scrambling for their things, asking a thousand questions such as 'Where is this to be put?' 'What shall we do for such and such a thing?' However, the hurry is pretty well over, the dust subsides, the clamours cease and I am hurried away to dress. I am really surprised at Smith's [the Delanys' housekeeper] thorough cleverness in going through her work. She has got everything almost in as much order as if she had been here a week." Later enlarged, with the addition of a splendid ballroom containing fine Adamesque plasterwork, Mount Panther survived until the late 1960s but has since fallen into ruinous condition.

Raphoe Palace
COUNTY DONEGAL

A date stone on Raphoe Palace advises that work on the building was begun in May 1636 and finished in August the following year. It was constructed at the behest of the then Bishop of the diocese, John Leslie. Born in Aberdeenshire in 1571, he spent two decades in Spain before returning to Britain where he became a favorite of James I, who made him a privy counsellor of Scotland. In 1628 he was appointed Bishop of the Isles, and five years later transferred to Raphoe where he found much of the Episcopal lands in lay hands but succeeded in regaining them. Bishop Leslie's combative nature became more apparent and more necessary after 1641 with the onset of the eleven-year Confederate Wars. He was a staunch royalist, and battled against both the Irish and Cromwell's Parliamentary army, for this reason becoming known as the "Fighting Bishop." Despite ultimately being on the losing side, he was permitted to remain in situ during the Commonwealth period. When Charles II was restored to the throne in 1660, Leslie—then aged 90— is said to have rode from Chester to London in order to pay homage to the king. As a reward for his unstinting loyalty, Charles II recommended the bishop to the Irish House of Commons, which voted him a gift of £2,000. By now transferred to the See of Clogher, he used this money to buy the Glaslough estate in County Monaghan. His descendants live there still, because at the age of 67 the bishop finally married, his bride being Catherine Cunningham, teenage daughter of the Dean of Raphoe: the couple had five children. Bishop Leslie died in 1671, aged 100. In 1838 Raphoe Palace was gutted by fire, and has remained a ruin ever since.

Castle Saunderson COUNTY CAVAN

Around the middle of the seventeenth century the land on which Castle Saunderson stands passed into the hands of one Robert Sanderson, previously a Colonel in the army of Gustavus Adolphus of Sweden. In 1675 the estate was inherited by his eldest son, another Colonel Robert who sat in the Irish House of Commons and married Jane Leslie, a daughter of the Right Reverend John Leslie, Bishop of Clogher. The couple had no children and so Castle Saunderson passed to a nephew, Alexander Sanderson. It was the latter's grandson, another Alexander, who changed the spelling of the family name to Saunderson as part of an ultimately fruitless effort to claim the Castleton peerage of the Saundersons of Saxby, Lincolnshire (the first and last Earl Castleton having died unmarried in 1723). In turn his son Francis built the core of the present house. Staunchly anti-Catholic, he is said to have disinherited his eldest son for

marrying a member of that faith (or it could have been because she was the daughter of a lodge keeper at Castle Saunderson). So the estate of over 12,000 acres went to a younger son, Alexander, who transformed what had been a classical residence into an Elizabethan-Gothic castle. He likewise disinherited his first-born son because he was crippled, and another son who proved rebellious, eventually leaving Castle Saunderson to the fourth son, Colonel Edward James Saunderson who, like his forebears, was a Whig politician, and in Ireland leader of the Liberal Unionist opposition to Gladstone's efforts to introduce some measure of Home Rule. It appears to have been after the death of his eldest son, Somerset Saunderson, in 1927 that the family moved out of the house, although they did not sell the property until half a century later. After being used as an hotel, Castle Saunderson was gutted by fire in the 1990s.

A fine triumphal arch and several lodges at points around the estate walls give an indication of how well Cloverhill must have looked when first enlarged to a design by Francis Johnston. But while the arch and lodges survive, albeit in various states of repair, the house which was once their raison d'être *has all but disappeared.*

Cloverhill COUNTY CAVAN

Looking at the building now, it is hard to imagine that half a century ago Cloverhill was one of the region's finest neoclassical villas. The original house, built in 1758 for James Sanderson and then called Drumcassidy, was a simple two-storey Georgian block, but in the late 1790s a descendant of the same name paid Francis Johnston £22 to design something smarter, the older residence being largely absorbed into the new. Born in Armagh in 1760, Johnston's talent was early recognized by the city's architecture-loving Archbishop Richard Robinson who encouraged the young man and his training. When Robinson's preferred architect Thomas Cooley died in 1784, Johnston became his successor and received a number of early commissions that established his reputation. Thereafter, he enjoyed a highly successful career, not least thanks to his versatility which meant he could design in the Gothic style (Charleville Forest, County Offaly) or the Classical (Townley Hall, County Louth). Cloverhill was an early example of the latter style. Now of three storeys—the third being concealed behind a wide limestone eaves cornice—the building was given an east-facing breakfront façade centered on a handsome pedimented Ionic portico. The south side was distinguished by a bow with tripartite windows. Offshoots of the family remained in residence until 1958 when, exactly 200 years after the house was first built, it was sold and thereafter gradually fell into ruin. Cloverhill is today a roofless shell, the portico seemingly removed more than two decades ago and installed on the front of another house in County Wexford.

Killeevan Glebe COUNTY MONAGHAN

According to the terms laid out in Ireland's Planning and Development Act of 2000, a protected structure "is a structure that a planning authority considers to be of special interest from an architectural, historical, archaeological, artistic, cultural, scientific, social or technical point of view. If you are the owner or occupier of a protected structure, you are required to prevent it becoming endangered, whether through damage or neglect." Each local council is legally obliged to compile a list of buildings within its area that are deemed to merit protection. Owners or occupiers of protected structures are in turn obliged to make sure that the building does not become endangered through neglect, decay, damage, or harm. Generally, if a structure is kept in habitable condition and regular maintenance is carried out (such as cleaning out gutters, repairing missing slates, repainting external timberwork) it should not become endangered. Unfortunately there is often a disparity between legislation and implementation as can be seen by the state of the glebe house at Killeevan, County Monaghan. The church where its occupant would have taken services stands close by and the core of this clerical residence is believed to date from c.1800: the handsome bow certainly suggests a date in the opening years of the nineteenth century. The house was described by Samuel Lewis in 1837 as a "neat building," but sadly that is no longer the case, despite the structure being included in the local council's list of protected structures.

Keen to encourage clergymen to live in their parishes and to discourage the holding of multiple benefices, in the early nineteenth century the Board of First Fruits built many fine glebe houses such as that at Killeevan, as here often set in agreeable and extensive grounds. Such circumstances helped to make sure occupants stayed put and attended to their parochial duties.

Downhill's location close to cliffs leaves it exposed to harsh winds whipping off the north Atlantic. Bishop Hervey did his best to alleviate these circumstances, writing enthusiastically—or perhaps delusionally—to one of his daughters that the house was "becoming elegance itself, with 300,000 trees…and almost as many pictures and statues within doors."

Downhill COUNTY DERRY

It was the intrepid Lady Mary Wortley Montagu who first proposed that "the world consists of men, women, and Herveys." So it has remained ever since, although the inspiration for Lady Mary's remark was, of course, that most mercurial creature of early eighteenth-century England and confidante of George II's spouse Caroline: John, Lord Hervey. The third of his four sons, Frederick Augustus Hervey, was born in 1730 and was not expected to inherit either the family title or lands. He therefore needed to find an alternative career and accordingly became an Anglican clergyman. Thanks to the intervention of his eldest brother George, who as second Earl of Bristol in 1766 was appointed Lord Lieutenant of Ireland (although he never visited the country), Frederick Augustus—already a royal chaplain—was appointed Bishop of Cloyne. A year later, aged only

38, he became Bishop of Derry and thus responsible for one of the richest Irish sees. In 1779 Frederick Augustus also inherited the family earldom, making him even wealthier. Somewhat eccentric—he was, after all, a Hervey—on one occasion he organized a curates' race along the sands of Downhill, County Derry, the winner being awarded benefices then vacant in his diocese. Architecture was among his many passions and, on the cliffs above those sands, he built an immense palace with magnificent interiors. All of this was lost, first during a disastrous fire in 1851 and then after the place was unroofed in the middle of the last century. The shell is now managed by the National Trust, also responsible for the still-standing Mussenden Temple built by the Earl-Bishop in the grounds of Downhill.

Magheramenagh Castle COUNTY FERMANAGH

Magheramenagh Castle belonged to a branch of the Johnston family who had moved from Scotland to this part of the country in the early seventeenth century. The estate was inherited in 1833 by James Johnston who, following his marriage five years later, commissioned from Dublin architect John Benjamin Keane a residence for his new bride. The building was much in the style then fashionable, a loose interpretation of Tudor Gothic indicated by the presence of blind gables, polygonal turrets, castellations, and finials. Once all faced in crisp limestone, the main entrance was to the north, the southern front looking down on the river Erne. A large conservatory occupied much of the eastern end of the building while the service wing stood to the west, an enfilade of four reception rooms occupying the space between. Ultimately neither Magheramenagh nor its architect had a happy ending. Keane's career was blighted by alcoholism, he fell into debt, and was imprisoned in Dublin's Marshalsea Gaol before dying in 1859. Subsequently James Johnston died in 1873 and Magheramenagh passed to his son Robert. He in turn died just nine years later, leaving the estate to his son James Cecil Johnston, then aged less than two. James Cecil would be killed at Gallipoli in August 1915 and Magheramenagh was then occupied by his widow and two young daughters. Unable to manage, they left the property in 1921 and it was bought as a residence for the local Roman Catholic priest, serving this purpose until the 1950s when abandoned and unroofed. Afterward a large part of the house was demolished: it can be seen what now remains on the site.

See House COUNTY CAVAN

The Tithe Wars of the 1830s are a lesser-known episode in Irish history. Tithes, a payment to support the religious establishment and its clergy, had existed in the pre-Reformation Roman Catholic Church but from the sixteenth century onward, this obligatory contribution went to the Church of Ireland even though its members always formed a minority of the country's population. The tithe payment was expected to represent ten percent of the value of certain kinds of agricultural produce. Prior to the Tithe Composition Act of 1823 it was possible to pay tithes in kind instead of in cash. Thereafter tithes were required to be monetary. Understandably the tax was much resented and, following the Roman Catholic Relief Act of 1829 (popularly known as Catholic Emancipation), came under sustained attack. Eventually in 1838 the Tithe Commutation Act for Ireland was passed: this reduced the amount due directly by about

a quarter and made the balance payable in rent to landlords who then passed on the funds to the relevant authorities. Tithes were finally abolished following the Irish Church Act of 1869, which disestablished the Church of Ireland. Astonishingly, during this troubled period, George de la Poer Beresford, Bishop of Kilmore, County Cavan since 1802, embarked on the construction of an immense new residence for himself. A bishop's palace already existed close to the site of the present building, described by John Wesley in 1787 as "fit for a nobleman." But not apparently fit for Bishop Beresford who, in the mid-1830s, commissioned its replacement from Dublin-born architect William Farrell. It remained an Episcopal residence until the beginning of the present century before passing into private hands. Although not a ruin, the See House, as it is known, has suffered from standing empty and unoccupied.

Shane's Castle COUNTY ANTRIM

As a young woman, the eighteenth century's most celebrated actress, Sarah Siddons had met and been befriended by the Hon. Henrietta Boyle, who subsequently married John, first Viscount O'Neill. Hence in 1783, when Mrs Siddons was performing at Dublin's Smock Alley Theatre, she traveled to County Antrim to spend time with her friends at Shane's Castle, their home on the banks of Lough Neagh. In her memoirs, she recalled the visit: "I have not words to describe the beauty and splendour of this enchanting place; which, I am sorry to say, has since been levelled to the earth by a tremendous fire. Here were often assembled all the talent, and rank, and beauty of Ireland… The luxury of this establishment almost inspired the recollections of an Arabian Night's entertainment. Six or eight carriages, with a numerous throng of lords and ladies on horseback, began the day by making excursions around this terrestrial paradise, returning home just in time to dress for dinner. The table was served with a profusion and elegance to which I have never seen anything comparable. The sideboards were decorated with adequate magnificence, on which appeared several immense silver flagons, containing claret. A fine band of musicians played during the whole of the repast. They were stationed in the corridors which led to a fine conservatory, where we plucked our dessert from numerous trees of the most exquisite fruits. The foot of the conservatory was washed by the waves of a superb lake, from which the cool and pleasant wind came, to murmur in concert with the harmony from the corridor." In 1816, while the castle was being renovated and extended to the designs of John Nash, it was gutted by fire and has remained a ruin ever since. Shane's Castle has been much used as a location during successive seasons of *Game of Thrones*.

In 1787 the Rev. Daniel Beaufort, a sociable Anglican clergyman and amateur architect, paid a visit to Shane's Castle and after enthusing over the splendid breakfast arrangements for guests, wrote that attached to the building was a "pretty and large theatre and magnificent ballroom 60 x 30, all of wood and canvas painted, and so sent ready made from London." It is believed that Mrs Siddons performed in this long-lost theater during her own visit some years earlier.

Further reading

The Irish country house has been the subject of many books (albeit often with the same properties repeatedly featured) and its ruins represent a subgenre of the category. Below are a few such works, as well as some others that help to explain the history of the Irish country house and its too-frequent decline.

Bence-Jones, Mark: *Burke's Guide to Country Houses, Volume I: Ireland* (Burke's, London, 1978, revised edition 1988)

Bence-Jones, Mark: *Twilight of the Ascendancy* (Constable, London, 1987)

Blake, Tarquin: *Abandoned Mansions of Ireland* (Collins Press, Cork, 2010)

Blake, Tarquin: *Abandoned Mansions of Ireland II* (Collins Press, Cork, 2012)

Dooley, Terence: *The Decline of the Big House in Ireland* (Wolfhound Press, Dublin, 2001)

Glin, Knight of, Griffin, D.J. and Robinson, N.K.: *Vanishing Country Houses of Ireland* (Irish Architectural Archive and Irish Georgian Society, Dublin, 1988)

Laffan, William: *Ancestral Interiors: Photographs of the Irish Country House by Patrick Prendergast* (Irish Architectural Archive, Dublin, 2010)

Marsden, Simon and McLaren, Duncan: *In Ruins: The Once Great Houses of Ireland* (HarperCollins, London, 1980)

Mulligan, Kevin V.: *Vain Transitory Splendours: The Irish Country House and the Art of John Nankivell* (Irish Georgian Society, Dublin, 2018)

O'Byrne, Robert: *The Irish Georgian Society: A Celebration* (Irish Georgian Society, Dublin, 2008).

Somerville-Large, Peter: *The Irish Country House: A Social History* (Sinclair-Stevenson, London 1995)

Index

Acknowledgments

The Irish Aesthete made its debut in September 2012. The blog was, and still is, a means of sharing my personal enthusiasm for Ireland's architectural heritage with as wide an audience as possible. From the start, the content has focused on historic buildings throughout the country, providing as much information about these as possible without being intimidatingly academic. The intention is to encourage interest, and ideally engagement, and thereby help ensure the conservation and preservation of our shared heritage.

I have been visiting houses around Ireland since I was an undergraduate at Trinity College, Dublin forty years ago. But prior to The Irish Aesthete I had never photographed any of them, indeed had never owned a camera. Once I began the blog, that obviously had to change—and it did, thanks to my phone. Month by month I taught myself how to take pictures, and how to improve the quality of those taken: it's still a learning process, not least because new phones regularly appear with better cameras.

Success on social media requires powerful and ample visual content, so there are always lots of pictures on the blog, critical in growing and sustaining an audience. Equally important is the regular and reliable production of new material. Since 2012 The Irish Aesthete has appeared three times weekly and developed an international following: it now averages 600-700 views per day. Followers are located all over the world, with the majority in English-speaking countries, Ireland, Britain, and the United States. The blog is linked to Irish Aesthete pages on Facebook, Twitter, Tumblr, and Pinterest so that everything also appears on them: as a result they attract similar numbers of followers, and feed back into the main blog. More recently The Irish Aesthete has established a strong presence on Instagram.

I am immensely grateful to everyone who follows or engages with The Irish Aesthete on any/all of these platforms, most especially anybody who comments and responds to postings. All writing is a solitary business and without feedback one could easily come to feel like a voice in the wilderness. Accordingly many thanks to all followers: your support has been invaluable. So also various tolerant friends and acquaintances pressed into service over the years to act as guides and companions on site visits around the country. While some places were already known to me, others were not, and they would probably have remained unexplored without my invaluable companions. Thanks also to Cindy Richards for having faith in this book, to Anna Galkina for her kind and sensitive editing, to Sally Powell for overseeing design, and to Geoff Borin for his design of the book: again, much gratitude to you all.

In spite of these contents suggesting otherwise, thankfully not every historic building in Ireland is a ruin. I would encourage an exploration of The Irish Aesthete across social media to gain a fuller sense of the richness of Ireland's wonderful architectural heritage. The more interest there is in the subject, the greater chance of it being cherished into the future.